Rachael Kable started her successful podcast, *The Mindful Kind*, in 2015 and it's already clocked up three million downloads and averages over 130,000 downloads per month. Her qualifications include a Bachelor of Psychological Science, a Graduate Certificate in Coaching and Counselling and an Advanced Certificate in Guiding and Teaching Meditation. She is a Melbourne-based mindfulness and meditation teacher.

The Mindful Kind

A meaningful
mindfulness guide
for wellbeing in the
modern world

RACHAEL KABLE

ABC
BOOKS

The ABC 'Wave' device is a trademark of the
Australian Broadcasting Corporation and is used
under licence by HarperCollins*Publishers* Australia.

First published in Australia in 2019
by HarperCollins*Publishers* Australia Pty Limited
ABN 36 009 913 517
harpercollins.com.au

HarperCollins*Publishers*
Level 13, 201 Elizabeth Street, Sydney NSW 2000, Australia
Unit D1, 63 Apollo Drive, Rosedale, Auckland 0632, New Zealand
A 53, Sector 57, Noida, UP, India
1 London Bridge Street, London, SE1 9GF, United Kingdom
Bay Adelaide Centre, East Tower, 22 Adelaide Street West, 41st floor, Toronto,
  Ontario M5H 4E3, Canada
195 Broadway, New York NY 10007, USA

A catalogue record for this book is available from the National Library of Australia

ISBN 978 0 7333 3953 0 (pbk)
ISBN 978 1 4607 1041 8 (ebook)

Cover design by Hazel Lam, HarperCollins Design Studio
Cover images and author photo by Declan O'Leary
Typeset in Minion Pro by Kirby Jones
Printed and bound in Australia by McPherson's Printing Group
The papers used by HarperCollins in the manufacture of this book are a natural, recyclable
product made from wood grown in sustainable plantation forests. The fibre source and
manufacturing processes meet recognised international environmental standards, and carry
certification.

CONTENTS

The Mindful Kind

Introduction

How often do you experience the present moment with a sense of openness and curiosity?

When you picked up this book, did you notice the colours on the cover and the weight of it in your hands? Did you hear the sound of the paper as you flicked to this page? Can you see the shapes of the letters, the blank areas, the perfectly rounded full stops?

Welcome to the world of mindfulness.

It's not a complicated world, nor a difficult one. Mindfulness is experiencing the present moment, without labels or judgement. It can be as simple as feeling a breath move in and out of your body or noticing the solid ground underneath your feet.

Yet how often do you find yourself 'out' of the present moment? Thinking about an upcoming work deadline while you're lying in bed at night? Writing a mental shopping list of the groceries you need to buy while you're doing a 'relaxing' yoga class? Eating dinner on a Sunday night and feeling a growing sense of dread as you imagine yourself going to work the following morning and opening up your email inbox?

Mindfulness itself may not be complicated or difficult, but it can still be challenging to practise. Many of us have been conditioned to worry about the future and ruminate over the past, so we regularly miss the present moment because our minds are tied up elsewhere. It can actually take a deliberate choice and effort to engage in mindfulness, but the more we do, the easier it can become.

As a teenager, I struggled regularly with stress, anxiety and low self-esteem. I felt unable to stop myself from thinking about things I regretted, or things I was worried about. I judged myself for being too shy, too short, too pimply, too boring, too stupid. Deep down, I knew I was making myself miserable and I also knew I was the only person who could change it.

In a bid to understand myself better, I decided to study psychology at university. The more I learned, the more passionate I felt about using my knowledge and skills to create a better life for myself and to work towards helping others do the same.

In my second year of study, I started volunteering on a helpline, and during the training I was taught a mindfulness technique. I felt a sudden moment of clarity; being mindful genuinely helped my erratic mind to slow down. I experienced a break from my stress and noticed a sense of calm and ease as I became more present in the moment.

Since that day, I've tried to implement mindfulness into my life in various ways. I started to practise mindful breathing when I couldn't sleep at night and used my senses deliberately during everyday activities, like cooking and showering. I encouraged myself to observe and explore different emotions, rather than chase happiness and avoid pain. I began to see the meaning in simple activities, like walking my dog or watering a plant, because they were opportunities to cultivate mindfulness when I would normally be lost in my thoughts.

Gradually, being more mindful changed my life in various, little ways that ultimately created big changes. I noticed benefits in my relationships, physical health and wellbeing, work and social media use. I had a greater sense of enjoyment of creative activities and hobbies. I felt more resilient and better equipped to manage my stress and anxiety. The nonjudgement I practised during mindfulness started translating into kinder self-talk, more open-mindedness towards others and less shame around my mistakes and shortcomings.

When I started talking about mindfulness on my podcast, *The Mindful Kind*, I received a multitude of messages from people who were noticing similar changes in themselves. I heard from a man in the US who began experiencing peaceful moments of reflection after many years of self-loathing and insecurity. A young woman sent me a comment via Instagram to explain how some slow mindful moments helped her experience a sense of calm acceptance after her partner was deployed in the armed services. I've heard from people experiencing grief, loneliness, physical pain and anxiety, who felt supported by their mindfulness practices.

I wrote this book because I wanted to share simple and meaningful ways for you to practise mindfulness that can easily be integrated into your everyday life. You'll discover mindfulness and meditation techniques to help relieve stress and anxiety, and practices to build your sense of overall wellbeing.

When I was studying, one of the strategies I learned was called the Wheel of Life. It was designed to help you discover which areas of your life need your attention. Basically, you draw a circle and divide it into sections (like a pizza), and you label each section with an important area of your life. For example, one section might be labelled 'self-care', another section might be 'work', another section might be 'hobbies and creativity', and so on. You then rate each section out of 10, based on how satisfied you are with it. For example, if you enjoy a number of fulfilling relationships, you might rate that section an 8 out of 10. If you feel as though you never have time for hobbies or creativity any more, you might rate that section a 2 out of 10.

I created this book with the hope that mindfulness can help you improve each important area of your life. I hope that Part Two about relationships will help you communicate better (and more mindfully!)

and deliberately foster more love and support. I hope that Part Four about health and wellbeing will help you practise mindfulness to experience better sleep, more meaningful exercise and mindful eating. I hope that by the end of this book, the rating for each little slice of your own Wheel of Life will be higher.

I recommend that you read through this book chapter by chapter, as each one builds on the last. However, if you find yourself experiencing a particularly stressful or overwhelming time, you can turn to the Appendix to find a collection of breathing techniques, mindfulness practices and meditations.

There's just one more thing to remember as you read this book. No mindfulness journey is exactly the same and I'd love you to try all these techniques with an open mind. Notice which ones resonate with you, work on those which challenge you, and allow your mindfulness or meditation practice to grow and evolve.

I hope you enjoy being part of The Mindful Kind.

With love,

Rach

PART ONE

Learning and Personal Growth

CHAPTER 1

Exploring outside your comfort zone

Imagine a safe and comfortable home. It's quiet and cosy, filled with all of your favourite things. You know your home so well that you could find your way around in the dark – and when it's stormy outside, it's the perfect place to take refuge.

Your comfort zone is just like your home. It's a secure place where you can stay within the boundaries and feel comfortable and safe.

However, we tend to enjoy exploring outside our homes, too. Without exploration, we grow bored and frustrated and isolated. We miss feeling the sunshine on our skin, the thrill of discovering new places, the challenges that arise from the unknown.

And the more we explore, the more we become familiar with new parts of the world. Initially, we might become familiar with our neighbourhood, then places we visit regularly (such as work, shops, school or friends' houses), then other states, or even different countries!

The same is true of our comfort zones. The further we explore outside them, the more our comfort zones expand. As the psychologist Abraham Maslow once said, 'In any given moment, we have two options: to step forward into growth or to step back into safety.'

Of course, stepping forward isn't always easy and neither will it guarantee success. For these reasons, I think it's incredibly important to focus on one thing: going outside your comfort zone will always teach you something. Perhaps it's not something you expect to be taught! You may find yourself learning from mistakes, feeling a range of challenging emotions, realising hard truths, or finding out more about yourself and your capabilities. You may even find yourself wishing you'd taken a different path or stayed within your comfort zone and it won't be until later that you can look back and feel grateful for making the choice to venture out there.

The temptation of a comfort zone

One of the main reasons why comfort zones are so alluring is that they tend to decrease stress. They offer a sense of safety and familiarity, so that when we return to them, we feel relieved. This is both a wonderful feature and a potential danger of comfort zones.

So how can we effectively use our comfort zones as safe spaces, while not becoming too attached and reliant on staying within them?

The answer lies in how you perceive them. Comfort zones, like homes, are safe and familiar, but in order to go exploring you need to leave them. If you can encourage yourself to see your comfort zone as a secure base to return to when you need it, but also a launching pad from which to boost yourself out, then you will be able to experience the safety of a comfort zone without needing to be there all the time.

Going outside my own comfort zone

In 2011, I moved away from my rural hometown to the second-largest city in the country so I could study psychology at university. Being an introvert who loved familiarity, it was completely outside my comfort zone. For several months, I struggled. I caught the wrong train in the middle of the night and ended up somewhere completely unknown. I felt overwhelmed by crowds and the hustle of city life. I pulled my car over to the side of the road (multiple times!), in tears, having taken a wrong turn and ended up somewhere unfamiliar.

Yet the thrill of being so far out of my comfort zone also pushed me to embrace the new. Within a few months, I'd mastered reading the train timetable and navigating around my area of the city. I'd discovered new support networks and felt safe even when things were unfamiliar. I learned to smile when I walked through crowds, just because it felt better than looking at the ground while ducking and weaving around people.

But it still wasn't easy to be outside my comfort zone. There were times when I felt knots of dread twisting and tightening in my stomach. There were mornings when I wanted to get in my car and drive back to my hometown. There were days when I wondered if I'd made a mistake moving to the city, where things were so different from the place where I'd grown up. There was even a period of several months when I became so judgemental about 'city life' that I spent the majority of my spare time daydreaming about moving back to the country. I had a detailed image of what my home would be like – far away from other people, with several dogs and a studio where I could dance – and I'd mentally created my garden, featuring winding, interconnecting paths and raspberry bushes in wooden boxes. I'd figured out how I would earn money in that remote location and I'd even gone so far as to start putting aside money to fund the dream.

However, this wasn't truly a dream; it was an escape. Rather than embracing the present moment and appreciating all the good things and opportunities in my life, I spent hours fantasising about something else. Of course, not having the perfect country house when I wanted it so badly created a real sense of sadness. I was constantly wishing for something I didn't have, believing that when I finally got it, everything would work out and I would be happy.

It was during this time that I began volunteering on a helpline at the Anxiety Recovery Centre for Victoria and I started learning about mindfulness. We were sitting in a room undergoing training and we were guided through the following mindfulness technique:

Bring your attention into the room.
Notice five things you can see.
Notice four things you can hear.
Notice three things you can feel.
Notice two things you can smell.
Notice one thing you can taste.

At the end of the technique, I felt content. By allowing myself to let go of the incessant daydreaming, as well as the predicting and planning that regularly contributed to my own stress, I'd learned what it felt like to simply be in the moment. No expectations. No judgement. Just an open-minded acceptance and curiosity about what that moment actually had to offer.

Mindfulness was completely new to me and a very different way of thinking and being. For such a simple practice, it often drew me so far out of my comfort zone that there were times I believed I couldn't do it.

My comfort zone was about always trying to stay a few steps ahead, so I could plan and predict my own future and avoid mistakes. It involved believing that happiness was in my future, when I would finally have everything I wanted. Inside my comfort zone, challenging and vulnerable emotions, such as anger and sadness, were bad. Happiness and excitement were good. Getting through tough times was about distraction and actively trying not to experience the present moment.

Mindfulness challenged all of that. My practice slowly began to teach me that I could allow my life to unfold and that I could embrace unpredictability, even when it was challenging. I discovered that my constant planning was causing more stress than providing help. I stopped suppressing emotions as much and found that by open-mindedly experiencing them, I felt less judgemental of myself and more self-compassionate. These shifts in thinking led to even more tangible benefits in my life, from better sleep to stronger relationships and more experiences of fun and creativity (more on that later!).

For now, it's important to understand that your comfort zone may be challenged by your mindfulness practice. And that's okay.

Mindfulness, stress and exploring the boundaries of your comfort zone

When we go exploring outside our comfort zones, we often experience varying degrees of stress. However, this isn't necessarily a bad thing! In fact, we can experience a state of 'optimal stress', a term coined by psychologist Robert Yerkes in 1907, which refers to a behavioural space in which we experience slightly higher stress than normal. This experience of slightly higher (but still manageable) stress leads to an increase in performance.[1]

For example, imagine you're asked to give a speech at a close friend's wedding. You agree, but you can already feel a tingle of fear starting to build. Your previous experiences of public speaking remind you of sweaty palms, stuttered words and a group of blank faces staring back at you with a hint of pity. So you start preparing. You write some notes, edit them, memorise some key points, practise your speech in front of someone else and create cue cards. When it's time to present your speech, you feel a rush of fear, but your preparation supports you through it and you end up feeling quite proud of how it unfolds.

Now, let's imagine the same situation but without the experience of optimal stress. Your friend asks you to present a speech at their wedding and while you're honoured to have been asked, you don't feel any stress about it. Maybe you haven't had any experiences with public speaking before and you believe it will all happen easily and naturally, without you having to put in any effort. So you don't prepare and you don't particularly think about it either. When the moment to present rolls around, you feel a sudden, overwhelming sense of unexpected fear and you don't know what to say.

Compared to the first scenario, the second scenario doesn't involve optimal stress and results in a decrease in performance.

While many of us perceive stress as a challenge, or a sign that something's wrong, there are actually some incredible benefits which can come from experiencing it. Not only can optimal stress increase your performance, it can also motivate you to work towards your goals, try new things and make beneficial changes in your life. Even the experience of stress itself can encourage you to discover new ways of managing it, so that when you do experience higher levels of stress or anxiety, you're equipped with different tools and techniques to support yourself through it.

Keep in mind that when you expand your comfort zone, you may experience some stress – and that can be a good thing! Allow it to become part of what motivates you and encourages you to grow. If you do find the stress starts to become overwhelming, remember that you can return to your comfort zone for a little while, use mindfulness techniques, or turn to your support network for help. On the next page you'll discover some helpful tips for going outside your comfort zone in small yet meaningful ways.

Tips and techniques for going outside your comfort zone

Seek support for particularly challenging journeys outside your comfort zone. Humans weren't made to traverse the wilderness alone! Don't be afraid to ask for help, create a buddy or accountability system, visit a health professional, join a support group or communicate with people you trust.

Try doing everyday things differently. Not every attempt to explore beyond your comfort zone has to push you to the edge of your boundaries. Why not practise – and make it a daily habit – to make small changes in your life, such as walking different routes, trying new recipes, listening to music you might not normally listen to, getting out of bed earlier (or later), swapping chores with someone else in your home, or using a different form of relaxation from what you would normally use.

Change 'I can't do it' to 'I can't do it, yet.' Such a simple change can completely alter your perceptions of your abilities and your potential to grow. By saying 'I can't do it, yet', you'll give yourself a chance to learn and gain knowledge (or skills), whereas 'I can't do it' implies that you already believe you never will.

Spend time with people who are different from you. A few of my friends are extroverted and I find it both challenging and rewarding to spend time with them. They show me new ways of interacting and communicating, while encouraging me to flex the boundaries of my introversion and learn more about myself.

Return to your comfort zone to recharge, or when you've gone beyond optimal stress. Remember how the comfort zone is like a home? Sometimes, you just need to be at home so you can feel safe and recharge your batteries and the same goes for your comfort zone. You don't need to be out of it all the time, or feel like you should always be pushing yourself! In fact, I think we all need decent breaks every now and again so we can reflect and re-energise. Return to your comfort zone when you need to and simply appreciate being there for a while.

Use affirmations. Choose a few simple affirmations you can repeat whenever you need a little boost of self-belief. For example, 'I am capable of exploring outside my comfort zone' or 'I am confident' or 'I love challenges which help me grow.' Of course, you can also create your own affirmations, too!

Do nothing. While this may seem like a simple activity, many of us just aren't used to doing nothing. Go somewhere quiet so you can be alone, put your phone away, turn off all technology, try not to fidget and just sit and do nothing for a few minutes. It may feel uncomfortable or disconcerting, and that's alright. If your mind starts racing, try to become present by noticing your breath or tuning in to your different senses. This practice is great if you're feeling nervous about going outside your comfort zone because it will likely challenge you without pushing you too far (plus, you can stop whenever you like).

Try not to 'just do it' before you feel ready. Going outside your comfort zone often takes courage, patience, kindness, self-efficacy and understanding. Sometimes, we put such high expectations on ourselves and want perfection, when we often need some time and self-care to adjust. Some days you may find it easy to explore outside your comfort zone, but other days might be really difficult. Always try to listen to what your body and mind are telling you and make adjustments accordingly.

Take your time in making decisions. When we make quick decisions, we tend to do the same things over and over again, or act on autopilot. The next time you need to make a decision, actually take some time to think about it and explore whether there might be a better way to go about it, or new things you could incorporate!

Go outside your comfort zone for yourself, not because other people think you should. At the end of the day, the choices you make and the actions you take need to come from a place of internal motivation, when you choose to go outside your comfort zone because you want to learn more and grow as a person for your own sake.

CHAPTER 2

The whole-hearted approach to mindfulness

People start their mindfulness journeys for their own reasons: to manage stress and anxiety, to cope with challenges in life, to find more serenity and relaxation – perhaps out of curiosity, to have a new experience, or simply by chance. But for whichever reason you're reading this book, you might find yourself facing challenges with your mindfulness practice every now and then.

The truth is, I don't always find mindfulness easy to practise. There have been times when it has triggered frustration and a sense of hopelessness, and other occasions when it has shaken me to my core. Being mindful has asked me to drop the layers of avoidance, judgement and inauthenticity that I built as a means of self-protection. It can feel incredibly daunting, embarrassing and scary, and it has sometimes made me feel very vulnerable.

I remember the first time I gave myself permission to actually experience sadness when I felt sad for no real reason. Rather than running from it, denying how I felt, or feeling guilty for being sad when I believed I shouldn't be (because life was good and I had a lot to be grateful for), I went to bed and lay down, letting myself cry. I didn't turn to the unhelpful coping mechanisms I'd used in the past: doing vigorous exercise, drinking alcohol, watching hours of television, or losing myself in a busy to-do list in order to numb the sadness I felt. I created a space to just feel sad, to cry and to refrain from judging myself about it.

I tried to be more curious about my experience – tuning in to my senses and noticing how the emotion felt in my body. I listened to the thoughts going through my mind and paid attention to my physical reactions to them.

After a little bit of time, I felt the emotion shifting. I no longer felt like I needed to cry, and the tension in my body softened a little. I realised that my belief system about sadness – that I needed to avoid it lest it take over – was false. I'd spent so much energy avoiding this emotion, thinking that it would lead to depression and an unhappy life. But I learned that I *was* capable of feeling sad and experiencing it fully, while also allowing it to pass with self-compassion and nonjudgement (if somewhat imperfectly!).

The whole-hearted approach to mindfulness isn't about becoming an eternally calm, understanding, compassionate and unwavering person. It doesn't represent the eradication of challenging emotions, like sadness, anger and feeling overwhelmed. And it isn't about learning to control your thoughts, reactions, feelings and behaviours.

The whole-hearted approach to mindfulness is knowing that you have the freedom to experience your life, just as it is. Remembering that there will be ups and downs, steps forward and back, bumps in the road and unforeseen challenges. You will experience pain and hardship, though it might be completely different from the pain and hardship experienced by someone else. It's also about becoming curious, rather than judgemental, towards your internal and external worlds. It means being open to change and being willing to learn and grow.

The whole-hearted approach to mindfulness is a journey towards more compassion, openness, presence and understanding within the context of a sometimes messy human life.

Terence's story

Terence was relatively new to the practice of mindfulness when he first connected with me. Just a few months prior, he had been drugged and assaulted by someone he knew. In the weeks that followed, he became more sick than he'd ever been in his life and was admitted to hospital, with the suspicion that he'd contracted a tropical disease. However, when his results came back, Terence was diagnosed with HIV.

His body was going through seroconversion, which occurs when the virus first takes hold of the body and people often experience flu-like symptoms. Fortunately, medications have come incredibly far in the last twenty years and Terence's life expectancy is the same as for someone without HIV. The medications also make it impossible for Terence to pass on the virus, or for him to get sick from it.

However, when he started taking the medication, Terence had to endure its severe side effects, losing 8 kilograms in three weeks. He had heard that the practice of mindfulness could help alleviate stress and strengthen resilience and he began to believe that practising mindfulness might help him. After searching on iTunes and listening to various podcasts, he came across *The Mindful Kind*.

Feeling as though he'd spent his adult life over-thinking and stressing about things that never happened, Terence started to implement my tips about mindfulness. Not only did he feel stronger and more confident, he also discovered a way to cope with his diagnosis. By bringing himself back into the present moment via breathing techniques and noticing his senses, he was able to stop negative thoughts from spiralling out of control into what he called a 'black hole'.

Terence also started experimenting with mindful eating: taking the time to be thankful for his food, savouring the flavours and appreciating the nutrients his body was receiving.

Despite the emotionally and physically draining journey Terence found himself on, he was also beginning to experience mindful moments and benefits from his practice. He felt like he was on his way to living a more mindful life, facing the world stronger and more aware than he had ever been before.

The techniques and practices you will learn throughout this book aren't meant to be done perfectly. They are for you to experiment with, to play with and to implement into your life in ways that are helpful or meaningful to you. Some days, your mindfulness practice will feel aligned, some days it will challenge you. Some days you'll feel motivated, some days you won't.

No matter what happens, please be kind. Not just towards others, but towards yourself. You might notice yourself thinking 'I am hopeless at these mindfulness techniques – my mind is far too busy' or 'I don't deserve to take a break and practise mindfulness when I'm stressed.' Notice these thoughts and give them a gentle challenge. Here are some of the reminders I've used over the years.

- My mind is going to wander during mindfulness practices, and that's okay. The more I bring it back, the stronger my mindfulness practice becomes.
- I deserve to take a few mindful moments for myself.
- Mindfulness isn't just about good experiences, it's important during challenges, too.

- My mindfulness practice doesn't need to be perfect.
- Mindful awareness helps me experience and appreciate my everyday life.
- A few minutes of mindfulness is more than nothing at all.
- I don't need to be calm to be mindful.
- I'm doing the best I can.

While the practice of mindfulness follows a few simple guidelines – being present in the moment, being nonjudgemental and acknowledging what's unfolding – there is a huge opportunity for individuality within these guidelines. Through practising mindfulness myself and connecting with hundreds of other people about their own practices, I've learned that there isn't one perfect way to be mindful.

Some people find mindfulness through quiet meditation. Others find it by immersing themselves in creative activities or hobbies. I've heard about all different kinds of mindful walking – people watching the sunrise, playing with their dogs, feeling the movements within their bodies, noticing their environments, having some time to tune in to their thoughts and feelings. Some people find mindfulness in cooking, or showering, or journaling, or taking photographs, or all of the above.

And that's because mindfulness isn't a practice you can only apply at certain times of the day and in particular situations. Mindfulness can be an attitude, a way of living life by connecting with the now and being open and curious about what there is to experience.

Like me, you may start with some of the more traditional mindfulness techniques, then expand your practice to encompass many different areas of your life. I quickly learned that tuning in to my senses wasn't just something I could do for two minutes each day during an intentional mindfulness practice, but something I could do at any time. I could check in with my sense of smell after lighting a scented candle, or when adding spices to a meal, or while washing my hair. I could notice the sensations within my body when I was sitting in the sunshine, or practising yoga, or patting my dog. I could look at all the different colours whizzing past me as I caught the train home from work, or look with gratitude at the objects in my home. I could listen to music, to the sounds of the morning as I woke up, to the oceanic sounds of my own breath. And I could really taste the flavours I came across, from my toothpaste to my coffee to the explosion of sweetness of a piece of fruit, or the subtle fusions of flavours within a bowl of soup.

I didn't just tune in to my senses – I discovered hundreds of tiny, rich and meaningful moments within my everyday life. I learned that there was so much more to be experienced and cherished at times when I had previously wished I was somewhere else, or someone else. Before learning about mindfulness, I constantly daydreamed about achieving my goals and having all the things I thought I wanted, not realising what I was missing out on in the moment.

It may take some time for you to find your way towards embracing mindfulness whole-heartedly, and even then, you may find yourself yo-yoing between mindful living and non-mindful habits. This is absolutely okay and normal – for many of us, it would be impossible to be mindful all of the time! Modern society is ripe with mindless distractions, judgement and comparison, and it often encourages us to want new things we don't have and to fantasise about the future. It's also healthy to reflect on the past and learn from mistakes, to think about the road ahead of us and to make goals.

So, how can we balance mindfulness with everything else that takes us out of the present moment?

I wish I could give you an answer to this question, but this is something you will need to explore for yourself. The more you practise mindfulness, the more you will see opportunities to be mindful each day and the stronger your practice will become. It's quite a natural progression and, once you get started, your mindfulness practice can continue to grow and grow.

I know it can be difficult to know where to begin. Throughout this book, you'll learn many different techniques, tips and strategies, but first here are three tips for starting a mindfulness practice and easing into whole-heartedness.

1: Start when you wake up in the morning

Choose one mindfulness practice and engage with it as soon as you wake up in the morning. You could tune in to all your senses, or just focus on one. You might like to follow the simple journey of your breath, flowing in and out. You could do a body scan, checking in with each part of your body and noticing how you feel physically. These are just a few ideas that I'll cover more in depth in later chapters. For now, just choose one simple mindfulness practice and continue to bring your focus back to it whenever your mind may wander.

For me, this strategy created a huge shift in the way I started my day. I used to hear my alarm go off, then immediately start counting down the time until I had to get up, while thinking about all the things I didn't want to do that day. Before my feet even hit the floor each morning, my stomach was knotted with anxiety and I could feel a sense of dread coursing through my body. It was often the worst few moments of my whole day.

Now I wake up in the morning and I immediately move my focus to the present moment: the feeling of the warm doona cocooning my body, the movement of my breath and the sounds outside the room. Rather than thinking myself into a spiral of anxiety, I trust in my ability to take the day as it comes and to embrace those morning moments with presence and appreciation.

It took a while before this became my norm, but it's one of the subtle yet incredibly powerful ways that mindfulness has made a positive difference in my everyday life.

2: Look at the world with childlike curiosity

The cultivation of a mindfulness practice doesn't need to be complicated or over-thought. It can be as simple as learning to let go of the 'adult lens' through which you see the world and rediscovering your childlike sense of wonder and curiosity. I believe that mindfulness is a way of being that we unlearn as we progress through life. We are taught to judge and apply labels and we often aren't encouraged to just be – instead, we're encouraged to focus on the future and compare ourselves to others.

But have you ever seen a child engaging in an activity just for the fun of it, with complete presence, nonjudgement and curiosity? This is the attitude I'd like you to uncover within yourself. Go for a walk (leaving all technology behind) and explore somewhere new, with a sense of excitement about not knowing what's around the next corner. Spend time with a friend and give them your full attention, as though they're the most important person in the world to you in that moment. Draw something and use colours that don't make sense, or go outside the lines and use your imagination.

This childlike curiosity is a gift and it's something we can learn to give back to ourselves. No pressure, no destination, no failure, no judgement. Just a genuine interest in experiencing and learning more about yourself and the world around you.

3: Use stress as a signal

Whenever I notice myself becoming stressed, I perceive it as a signal to engage in a mindfulness technique. The rushing thoughts, racing heart, sweaty palms and knotted stomach are like road signs pointing me back towards mindfulness and self-care. I might schedule in some time for a mindful activity, such as walking, taking a bath or doing yoga. If I'm really short on time, I'll try to use any small opportunities to practise mindful breathing techniques for a few seconds or minutes.

Below, you'll find two simple breathing techniques – the point of stillness and three-part breathing. These techniques can be used at any time when you notice stress building, such as before an interview, when your to-do list feels overwhelming, if you receive an unexpected expense, or when you'd like to let go of spiralling thoughts.

The point of stillness

Take a few moments to bring your attention into the now, perhaps checking in with your own thoughts and feelings and the world around you. You might notice sounds, sights, tastes or smells, and various sensations (such as the texture of materials against your skin). When it feels right for you, move your focus to your breath, just noticing as it flows in and out of your body.

Begin paying attention to the natural pause at the end of each exhale: the point of stillness. You don't need to elongate this pause or change it in any way, just notice its presence.

Continue with this practice as long as you like, perhaps a few minutes, or a little longer. Your mind will likely wander (and that's perfectly okay!), so gently refocus on the practice whenever you can.

Three-part breathing

Unlike the point of stillness, this breathing technique involves changing the breath (and therefore isn't technically mindful, but it can still be a wonderfully calming practice).

Take a deep breath in and hold it for a brief moment, then allow approximately 30 per cent of your breath to be exhaled from your stomach area. Hold the breath for another brief moment, then exhale another 30 per cent of the breath from your rib area. Hold the breath once more and exhale the remainder of your breath from your chest area.

It may take a few breaths before you find the right balance for exhaling in three different parts, which is one of the reasons why I find it such a powerful way to bring my attention into the moment!

Again, you can enjoy this technique for as long as you like, bringing your mind back any time you notice it has wandered away.

Potential benefits of mindfulness

As more research is conducted in the area of mindfulness, the benefits of this practice are becoming clearer and more widely recognised. One of various studies showing a reduction in stress was conducted at Massachusetts General Hospital in 2013, which included ninety-three individuals with generalised anxiety disorder. The participants were randomly assigned to either a mindfulness-based stress reduction (MBSR) therapy group or an active control group who didn't receive mindfulness training. After eight weeks, participants who received MBSR training showed a significant reduction in anxiety and stress and an increase in positive self-statements, which may also indicate better resilience in the face of challenges.[1]

In 2010, a previous study showed that after just four days of mindfulness training, participants with no prior meditation experience showed an improvement in mood and reduced fatigue and anxiety. They also showed a significant improvement in visuospatial processing, working memory and executive functioning, suggesting that even short periods of mindfulness training can help improve cognition.[2]

In a study published in 2015, more than two thousand participants who had experienced three or more previous major depressive episodes were randomly assigned to either mindfulness-based cognitive therapy (MBCT) or maintenance anti-depressants. Over a 24-month period, all participants were followed up on five separate occasions. The results showed that MBCT was just as effective for the prevention of depression as anti-depressant medication.[3]

I asked some of my mindfulness clients about how mindfulness has been of benefit to them, and this is what they answered:

Christina: Mindfulness has helped me stay longer in the present moment, to breathe more deeply, to worry less about things I cannot change and to become more grateful.

Simone: Using mindfulness has helped me achieve some major physical challenges, such as running a half-marathon and hiking Mount Bogong. When I was struggling and exhausted, rather than focusing on what was ahead of me and how far I had to go, I used mindfulness to bring my attention back to each and every step I was taking, and took deep inhales and exhales. Treating each step forward as a small achievement towards the bigger goal had me over the finish line and at the summit before I knew it.

Mindfulness also played a large part in helping me heal when I suffered a miscarriage. I was so hard on myself to get over it and move on, but I decided to practise mindfulness and let myself accept and experience the emotions I was going through, rather than trying to suppress them and force myself to feel better. I also realised that it was important for me to do things which I love – the things we don't necessarily dedicate time to when we prioritise our responsibilities instead. I started putting effort into my passion projects, which then enabled me to leave a part-time job I wasn't enjoying and start up my own business working from home – what I now consider my dream job. So when I say mindfulness has changed my life, I really do mean it. It has helped me wake up every morning and feel more genuinely excited about my day ahead.

Emily: Before I discovered mindfulness, I was often feeling stressed, anxious and worried. I tended to be very pessimistic and used a lot of negative self-talk. I first heard about mindfulness when an old co-worker posted about Rachael's podcast, *The Mindful Kind*, on Instagram. I was curious, so I decided to check it out and listen to the first episode. Using Rachael's tips and advice, I started to slowly integrate some mindful practices into my life. I feel like my mindfulness journey has a long way to go, and I still have a lot to learn, but already I have started to see some of the benefits such as stronger relationships with my loved ones, reduced stress levels, and more gratitude for the present moment.

Claudia: My last relationship was, in short, what you could call a 'toxic relationship'. While all of my friends noticed that it wasn't good for me, I didn't. When I finally found the strength to end the relationship, thanks to my supportive environment, I felt more lost than I ever had before. Not only was I deeply hurt because I had been so in love, but I also felt like I didn't know myself any more: my goals, my interests, my passions. Then I found *The Mindful Kind* podcast episode on using mindfulness when dealing with break-ups. I learned that it was okay to feel all my emotions and cope better with them – that I didn't need to ignore them or push them away. Eventually, I felt able to move on.

You'll find more stories from Christina, Simone, Emily and Claudia throughout this book, including how mindfulness has helped them manage stress at work, cook mindfully and communicate more clearly.

If there's one thing I'd like to say about the mindfulness journey ahead of you, it's that I feel excited for you. I believe that mindfulness can have a meaningful impact for people in such individual ways and it still delights and surprises me when I hear about new ways that mindfulness has made a difference for someone. I hope that one day you can add your own list of benefits and positive experiences.

CHAPTER 3

Journaling techniques and inspiring prompts

I couldn't tell you how many hours upon hours I spent journaling when I was a young girl. I started keeping my first real journal when I was eleven years old and had filled it by the following year. I still have it, even though the pages fall out and I cringe every time I read it! However, it's clear just how important that journal was to me and how it gave me a nonjudgemental friend to talk to.

My next journal wasn't quite so innocent! Having just started high school and documenting those first tumultuous and emotional years, my journal became less of a venting method and more of a tirade of confessions. I wrote down all the thoughts I felt guilty to be thinking, the anxieties I kept bottled up and the mistakes I deemed myself to have made. It's honestly quite difficult to look back on and I've seriously considered burning it several times. Again, it's clear what the second journal meant to me. It was a comfort in times when I felt alone and something I could rely on to share the parts of myself I felt ashamed of. It was a sounding board for new ideas and hopes for the future and a space to detangle my confused thoughts.

These days, I use a variety of journaling methods. When I'm feeling overwhelmed, I like to write freely for about ten minutes to help me 'download' the thoughts and feelings onto paper (where they often make more sense!). Each day, I write down one simple memory I would like to remember. I also have a number of journals with prompts, including gratitude journals, list-making journals and daily prompt journals. In this chapter, you'll discover some of the benefits of writing, including fun and meaningful journaling techniques, and important times of your life when journaling could be especially useful.

The benefits of writing

With thousands of thoughts swirling around in our minds every single day, it's not surprising that writing can be a useful method of making sense of it all. The practice of journaling has been used by famous authors, inventors, visionaries and artists alike, including Charles Darwin, Albert Einstein, Leonardo da Vinci, Sylvia Plath and Thomas Edison – to name a few!

Being able to clarify your thoughts and feelings in a journal can be incredibly cathartic, while also providing an opportunity for personal growth. You can use journaling to encourage better productivity, more creativity and greater self-reflection. It can also help you make sense of challenging thoughts, record important events and become more organised. Research has shown that journaling can facilitate the expression of traumas and stress, aiding in the healing of emotional wounds and thereby decreasing stress.

The potential benefits are in abundance and with so many different techniques and journals to use, all you need to do is decide which type of journaling practice will best incorporate into your life and then just start writing!

Fun, meaningful and easy journaling techniques

Vision journaling

Several years ago, I decided to create a vision board. Essentially, a vision board is a large collection of all your goals, represented by pictures and quotes and any other inspirational material you might find useful. I loved the idea of it, but once I started, I realised that I didn't enjoy creating something so big and so final. I wanted something I could update and change, which I'd also be able to work on easily, even if I didn't have a lot of space.

Then I had the idea to buy a little, A5 blank notebook and start filling each page with all the things I'd wanted to put on a vision board. I created a page for holidays I'd like to go on, a page about what I wanted my book to be like (several years before I even started writing this book you're reading now), and a page about the type of dog my partner and I wanted and all the fun things we would do together (again, this was months before we even found our little dog, Moose – and there's a photo of a dog in my vision book which looks just like him. There's even a page about delicious teas!

Creating a vision book helped me become much clearer on what I wanted in my life. Not just things, but moments and adventures and feelings. It helped guide me as I moved forward and it's been such a fun and creative activity, which has become even more meaningful as time has passed and things have actually come to fruition. I start new pages whenever the inspiration hits and look back on things I used to want, but perhaps don't any more. My vision book has become a tool I use to look forward and also a keepsake of past goals and ideas.

Free-flow writing

This is a great journaling practice because it also incorporates mindfulness and allows you to develop your sense of nonjudgement.

Simply grab a pen and a piece of paper, then set a timer for five or ten minutes and just write.

You can write about your thoughts and feelings in that moment or you could write about the environment around you. Maybe you could explore each of your senses and describe each part of your body and how it's all feeling.

As you write, try to focus on observing and exploring, rather than judging or labelling.

At the end of the writing session, you could even just throw the pages away so you don't feel pressure to say the 'right' thing or maintain neat handwriting.

Gratitude journaling

You could purchase a gratitude journal – there are quite a few options available – or you could grab a blank notebook and then include any of the following prompts that resonate with you:

- List five people you're grateful for and why.
- Write about an experience you're grateful to have had.
- Describe what gratitude feels like.
- List ten things you own that make your life more fun.
- Name ten books/movies/television shows you're glad to have read/seen, and why!
- Write about a challenging experience you learned from (and how the lessons helped you in the future).
- Describe three features of your body you're grateful for.
- What can you appreciate about your day so far?

Choose a journal to guide you

There are so, so many wonderful journals available and, actually, the hardest part for me has nothing to do with *finding* a great journal and more to do with *choosing* the right one. I now have several different journals that I write in occasionally, including a planner where I write all my important dates, a notebook in which I write freely every week or so, and a daily journal that I use as a to-do list and habit tracker and in which I also write down one memory I want to remember for each day. It may sound like a lot of journals but I love to write and I enjoy using all these journals and journaling methods for different reasons.

I highly encourage you to think about what's important to you when you're choosing a journal to help guide your practice. Would you like big, blank pages where you can draw and make bullet points? Would you like plenty of prompts? What do you most want to keep track of – and does the journal make it easy for you to do that? Is the journal going to be too overwhelming? Does the journal inspire you to work towards goals that are really meaningful to you?

Once you find the journal which resonates the most with you, find a regular time to use it and keep it somewhere you will see it and be reminded to write in it.

List making

Using a list style when writing can be simple and quick to do, which makes it a great journaling technique for anyone who may be short on time! Simply find a blank journal, create some prompts for yourself (or find some on the internet) and write for as long as you like.

Here are a few simple lists you could try.

The fun and joy list
- Five things that brought me joy today.
- Three fun things I did last weekend.
- Ten things in my home that I'm happy to have.
- Three people I always have fun with.
- Five memories which make me smile.

The goals list

- One of my proudest achievements this year.
- Three goals I'm working towards.
- Ten things I've achieved in the past.
- Three rewards I can give myself when I achieve my goals.
- Five goals I'd like to set.

The mindfulness list

- Five different colours I can see around me.
- One emotion I'm feeling.
- Three sounds I can hear.
- Five things I can notice about my breath.
- Ten sensations I can feel in my body.

The favourites list

- Three songs I love.
- Five of my favourite movies.
- Three books I couldn't put down.
- Ten of my favourite places to visit.
- Three items of clothing I most enjoy wearing.

Whip out your journal ...

... *when you're struggling to fall asleep*

It's 11.30 pm. You've been hoping and wishing and wanting to fall asleep for the last hour, but all that seems to do is heighten your sense of frustration. Your thoughts are playing a game of whack-a-mole, appearing and disappearing, appearing and disappearing. You've tried every trick you know to help you drift off, but nothing seems to be working.

Why not give journaling a try? By downloading your thoughts onto paper, not only will you allow them to be acknowledged (thereby often reducing their repetitiveness and intrusiveness), but you can also write down anything that might actually be important to remember.

Write freely, without limitations, restriction or judgement, until you might just start to feel less overwhelmed and frustrated. When you're ready, put your journal away, turn off the light, do a breathing technique and see whether you can drift off more easily.

... *after finishing work for the day*

Many people who have written to me about their work felt unable to 'switch off' when it was over. They would take their work home with them – physically, mentally or both – and wonder why they never felt relaxed and focused on their home life.

Those feelings are understandable for many reasons: pressure to succeed, tight deadlines, over-commitments and being ever-reachable thanks to phones and emails. However, there is one simple trick that can make a huge difference – and that's journaling.

At the end of the working day, try to put aside five minutes to write down the main things you've been working on, items on your to-do list, thoughts and ideas you want to remember for the next day, emotions and important thoughts, struggles, who you can ask for support, and new ways of working smarter instead of harder.

Place all those important thoughts onto paper and keep it somewhere safe, so you can refer back to it the next day without forgetting the new things you might have learned from the previous working day.

... *when your emotions feel overwhelming*

A journal is a brilliant tool for emotional expression. It offers a safe space to explore emotions, to understand them and to learn more about them.

You may even notice your emotions adhering to patterns, or that certain emotions are triggered by regular events.

This greater understanding of your emotions can be helpful for a few different reasons:

1. You can identify times when you tend to feel more emotionally vulnerable and ask for support in advance, or schedule extra self-care.

2. You can learn more about what triggers certain emotions. For example, you might notice that on Thursday nights you feel particularly low and often end up arguing with your partner. At first, you might think it's just coincidence, but the more it happens, the more you notice a pattern. After some reflection, you realise that you usually go to bed an hour later on Wednesday nights because your favourite television show is on. You decide to record the show, rather than stay up late to watch it and notice that when you write in your journal on the next Thursday night, you don't feel as low as you normally would.

3. You can demonstrate to yourself just how much your emotions ebb and flow. As someone who used to wish happiness would last forever and who would feel like a failure every time I experienced sadness, learning that my emotions were always changing was both empowering and a relief! I came to understand that it was normal to have times of anger, sadness and being overwhelmed, and knew that those feelings would pass. It also enabled me to enjoy my happier emotions, rather than worry when they would end.

You may even like to keep a mood journal to gain a more thorough understanding of your emotions and how they change. Simply follow these prompts daily for at least a month and see what you can learn.

Date:

Day of the week:

Time:

Hours of sleep last night:

Food and drink consumed recently:

Challenging external events in the last twenty-four hours:

Challenging external events in the next twenty-four hours:

Persistent thoughts:

Description of mood:

... *on special occasions*

Another great opportunity to journal is on special occasions, such as your birthday or the start of a new year. You can simply write about your meaningful memories of that time, or create a snapshot of your life.

Some prompts you could answer include:

- your favourite song
- a hobby you enjoy
- the last person you hugged
- what the weather is like
- the headline of a newspaper or magazine
- your plans for the next weekend.

Here are a few prompts (and answers!) from a journal entry I shared on my blog for my birthday in 2017:

A meaningful memory from today: Going out for lunch at a great
café with my wonderful colleagues.

What I'm reading: *Unthink* by Chris Paley.

Three things on my to-do list: Take a bath, upload episode 83 of
The Mindful Kind podcast and pack for our trip to Sydney.

Something I do for fun: Taking flat-lay photos and reading books.
A new skill I'd like to learn: How to knit.

Tips and tricks for keeping a journal consistently

One of the biggest challenges people tend to face when keeping a journal is remembering to write consistently. Below, you'll find a list of helpful tips and tricks to assist you as you create a regular journaling practice.

- Write at the same time each day.
- Keep your journal somewhere obvious, such as next to your bed.
- Set a reminder on your phone.
- Write short entries and build up your practice as your confidence grows.
- Find a way to journal which is enjoyable to you. For example, you could draw instead of write, use stickers and colours, or write in dot-points.
- Let go of judgements; try not to criticise your handwriting or things you've written.
- Think of your journal as a friend you can check in with each day.
- Track things that are important and helpful for you so it feels more meaningful.
- Use a journal with dates pre-written on the pages to help yourself stay accountable.

And remember that this practice is for you! Tailor it to suit your lifestyle, time restraints, writing preferences and favourite journaling techniques.

PART TWO

Relationships

CHAPTER 4

Powerful communication skills

For a long time, I tiptoed around communication like it was a sleeping bear who would wake up and attack me with the slightest misstep. I didn't just avoid communication; I was terrified of it.

I often worried I would say the wrong thing, or that I wouldn't have time to create the 'right' response. Whenever a conversation didn't go the way I planned, my anxiety skyrocketed and I found myself later ruminating over things I'd said. There were times when the outcome of conversations made me feel physically sick. My stomach would be tied up in knots and if the anxiety lasted long enough, I'd end up with a pounding headache.

I remember lying to my parents about brushing my teeth when I was a little girl. I hadn't brushed them and panicked that I would be in trouble, so I quickly said I did. We'd just come home from a trip away and since my toothbrush was still packed in the car, I got in trouble anyway because I'd lied. Growing up, many of my experiences with communication were like that; I panicked, I lied, I said the wrong things, I regretted what I did say, I wished I'd never opened my mouth. I became fixated on communication and the things I'd said and the more fixated I became, the more I felt like I was getting it wrong. I grew hypervigilant about it and something as small as making a joke which no one laughed at became a really big deal for me.

Learning to communicate more mindfully didn't come naturally to me and it's something I still struggle with at times! However, the more I've practised communicating and implementing the key pillars of mindful communication, the richer my relationships have become and the more I've been able to understand and express myself. Not only has this been an incredibly cathartic process, but it's also helped me to release anxiety and move forward.

Communication is an incredibly powerful skill and by intertwining it with mindfulness practices, it can become an even more meaningful and transformational experience. We can learn more about ourselves and how to express our thoughts and feelings, while becoming more empathetic and patient towards other people's responses.

Emily's story

Emily's fiancé was in a car accident in mid-2017 and couldn't return to work for almost a year because of the effects of his concussion. Although her partner received a small income from being on medical leave, Emily became largely responsible for supporting them both. She was worried about their finances and knew they needed to reduce their expenses, do some serious budgeting and put money aside for their upcoming wedding. Emily was dreading having the conversation, feeling awkward and uncomfortable, and not wanting to cause her fiancé to feel guiltier than he already did.

They decided to set aside a time to talk and Emily ensured there weren't any distractions, such as phones or television. Emily focused on mindfully listening to her fiancé and his concerns; she slowed down her impulsive reactions and considered how she really wanted to respond (instead of blurting things out) and how to express how she was truly feeling. After the conversation, they both felt supported by each other and confident with their financial plan.

Shortly after, Emily once again used mindfulness to express herself during an important conversation. She and her fiancé were feeling the pressure of everyone else's opinions on their upcoming wedding, particularly those of Emily's future mother-in-law. Emily and her fiancé decided to chat with her about their wedding planning in the hope that they could respectfully let her know they wanted to make their own choices, but that they would turn to her for advice if they needed it! Fortunately, Emily's future mother-in-law was open to their communication and understood their opinions. Being mindful, calm and respectful in this situation enabled Emily and her fiancé to share their ideas and desires clearly and maintain a positive relationship with someone they both cared for.

The six key pillars of mindful communication

I'm going to share my six key pillars of mindful communication with you and I really encourage you to infuse them into your relationships. They outline a simple guide for approaching communication in an honest, mindful and respectful way. You can use them in conversations with loved ones, colleagues, friends or anyone else you might speak with in day-to-day life.

First of all, though, a cautionary word: this process might take time and it isn't always predictable! You could be the perfect communicator and still a conversation might take an unexpected turn and become a challenging experience. For example, Emily's future mother-in-law could have taken offence to their request and become angry, upset or sad. Communication isn't always easy and it might not go to plan because you can't control how someone else will react, even when you're as respectful as possible. That's okay! You haven't failed, or done the wrong thing. You're still learning and growing, as are the people around you. Try to embrace any challenges in your communication attempts as opportunities to build your resilience and practise vocalising your thoughts and feelings in an empathetic and honest way.

If you notice yourself thinking that you've made a big mistake and you should never have even tried to communicate, ask for some time away from the conversation so you can think about and process what's unfolding. If you're at all like me, you'll likely feel quite overwhelmed when communication doesn't go the way you planned and it can be really worthwhile to have some space and time to think about it. Be gentle in asking for this space. You could say, for example, 'I'm feeling challenged by this conversation at the moment and I'd like to take some time to think about it before we continue.' Go somewhere you feel comfortable, do a mindfulness practice to help you feel more calm (I tend to gravitate towards breathing practices in these situations) and take your time to think about your intention for the conversation, what you could do to express yourself clearly and how you could reapproach the situation.

Usually, when the emotions begin to lessen, you'll probably be able to see the best way to proceed. It might involve writing down your thoughts because it's just too difficult to express them aloud. You might decide to apologise because something you said didn't sound the way you intended. Perhaps, you'll discover a better or clearer way of saying what you want to say!

Now let's take a look at the key pillars.

Pillar One: *Understand yourself and your needs*

The first difficulty I had with communication was that I didn't take the time to really listen to my own thoughts and emotions, and therefore I couldn't express my needs. Instead, I said 'I'm fine' whenever anyone asked me if I was okay (even when I wasn't), and I spent a lot of time avoiding my inner self by losing myself in books and television and over-committing to work and study. It wasn't just that I didn't want to talk about how I was thinking and feeling; it was that I didn't even want to admit it to myself.

Sometimes, it's hard to acknowledge when we're feeling sad or angry or stressed. So we bottle those emotions up and hope that they will go away, but they usually don't. Those emotions might fade into the background for a little while; they may even seem like they've disappeared altogether! But, inevitably, they'll return and you might end up feeling like there's something wrong with you.

Let me tell you something, something that totally changed both my life and how I dealt with vulnerable emotions.

There is *nothing wrong* with feeling sad, angry, stressed, frustrated, hurt or lonely.

There is *nothing wrong* with feeling however you might be feeling.

You are not broken or uncool or strange or stupid. You are a human being.

The truth is we all feel a huge range of emotions. You feel them, I feel them, your friends feel them, the people you admire feel them, celebrities feel them, your colleagues (or classmates) feel them. The vast majority of the people you've ever met in your whole life feel them.

Something important to remember about emotions is that they can be incredibly complex. I'm going to take you on a quick tour through the history of emotions so you can see a few things we've learned about emotions so far. In 1885, two scholars named William James and Carl Lange independently proposed that emotions occur because of how we interpret bodily reactions.[1] So, for example, if you're standing on top of a tall building and your heart starts to race, you might interpret this reaction as fear. Basically, their idea was that physical sensations needed to occur in order to experience the emotion. One of the problems with this theory is that research has since shown that people can still experience emotions without the presence of physical reactions. Also, electrical stimulation applied to the same physical site can trigger different emotions, which implies that there is more to emotions than just their physiological component.

About fifty years later, Walter Cannon and Philip Bard developed a new theory that the body felt an emotion and the brain identified it as an emotion at the same time.[2] They thought that physical reactions and emotions occurred simultaneously as a result of an external event. So if you dropped a glass that shattered all over the floor, you would have felt the emotion of anger at the same time as the physical sensations (such as flushing skin and frowning). The main issue with this theory is that it doesn't take into account the fact that we do sometimes feel emotions as a result of physical sensations. For example, some research has shown that by making yourself smile or laugh, you can actually trigger emotions of happiness and joy.

Then, in 1962, American scientists Stanley Schachter and Jerome Singer came up with a new theory that stated that we label our emotions based on physiological and environmental cues.[3] For example, if you're about to give a presentation at work and you feel your hands trembling, you might conclude that you feel nervous. However, if you're about to go skydiving, you might label that same physical sensation of trembling hands as a sign of excitement. This theory has also received its share of criticism; for example, sometimes we don't think about emotions before we experience them.

Research is still continuing in the area of emotions and I think this is important to know for two reasons: first of all, emotions are difficult to understand and they're often very individualised as a result of life experiences, environment, beliefs and values. It's taken scientists many years to even begin to understand emotions, so why do we put so much pressure on ourselves to know and control them?

And second, you can't be held accountable for your emotions. It is not often within our control to feel a certain way, and actually pursuing just one emotion (like happiness) can be harmful because it can lead to addiction, frustration, depression and other mental health challenges. However, what we do need to take responsibility for is how we *act* on our emotions. It's one thing to feel angry and another thing to act on that anger in a way that might be hurtful to others.

Experiencing a range of emotions in life is incredibly normal and, in many ways, can enhance your emotional intelligence. The more you can feel emotions and recognise them, manage them appropriately and increase your understanding of them (for both yourself and others), usually the higher your emotional intelligence will be.

With all that in mind, what are you feeling right now (honestly)? Take a moment to think about it, or perhaps even write down a list. For example, are you feeling curious to find out more about your emotions? Are you reading this book on your way to work and feeling nervous or stressed about the day ahead? Are you feeling content and satisfied? Maybe you're feeling a mixture of all these emotions, and more!

Now, what could support you through the experience of your emotions? Again, take some time to think about the question, or make some notes to dive into it a little more. For example, 'I'm feeling a bit frustrated because I set the goal to meditate each day and I keep forgetting or running out of time. I could ask my friend who loves meditating to share some tips with me and ask a family member to meditate with me, so I'll be less likely to forget! To help myself feel frustration and allow it to pass, I'll take some deep breaths and go for a walk in nature.'

Once you've explored your emotions and thought about what could support you through your experiences of them, actually go and ask people who might be able to help you. These people might include: a caring family member, a friend, a teacher, a colleague, a counsellor, a coach or a close neighbour. Alternatively, you could try finding a support group or calling a helpline.

Pillar Two: No one's a mind reader

I avoided eating with my sister for many years because she loves to share food. She'll double dip, take things from various plates and put things back if she doesn't want them any more. I, on the other hand, don't like to share. I like having my own plate and I don't really enjoy eating things other people have touched. My sister and I used to end up arguing because I assumed she knew I didn't like to share and she assumed that I did like to share. When I finally told her that I don't like sharing food, it was like a lightbulb went off. We both finally understood where the other was coming from and could set some new boundaries so we were both able to do what we wanted without annoying each other!

Challenges arise because we often assume that everyone thinks the same way we do and have similar beliefs, fears, likes and values. But we don't.

There were many times in a past relationship when I would ask my then-boyfriend if he could do the dishes (since I'd cooked), and if he forgot, I'd feel annoyed and do them myself. I assumed that he knew I was annoyed about having to do the dishes. He assumed that I didn't mind doing the dishes after all. I knew I was being passive aggressive, but I honestly thought he'd get the point and offer to help.

All the little instances like these eventually led me to the realisation that *no one can read my mind*. And, actually, no one should even have to try because it's my responsibility to be open and honest in the first place. Even though I still find it challenging to share my thoughts sometimes, I know that it's worthwhile because the more I've taken the responsibility to share, the easier my relationships have become. My loved ones don't have to guess how to help and support me because I can just ask (nicely!). My frustration doesn't slowly build and eventually tip over boiling point, causing friction and disagreements. I no longer keep my real thoughts about important things to myself, which often used to weaken my connections with others because they didn't get to know the real me.

And the same works in reverse. I enjoy knowing how my loved ones feel so I can help them out as best I can. It's great not having to guess why other people might feel frustrated or annoyed with me. With open channels of communication, I feel as though I more deeply know and understand those around me, and the connections between us are stronger than they've ever been.

Learning that no one is a mind reader is a big step, but then we also need to learn to communicate effectively, which flows nicely into the next pillar of mindful communication.

Pillar Three: Honesty and assertiveness

I'll never forget the time I bought a pair of overalls and within a week, most of the buttons had fallen off. I put it all into a bag (luckily, I still had the receipt) and took it back to the store. I was nervous, but I went up to the counter and explained what had happened. The assistant apologised and refunded my money.

It felt *amazing*. I know this may not sound like a huge deal, but being assertive in this way was not at all comfortable for me. When I was younger, I once ate a cold pie (which was supposed to be a hot pie!) because I felt guilty about asking the waiter to heat it up. I played piano for years as a child because I was too afraid to say I didn't want to do it. And once, I was in the back seat of a car that hit gravel and rolled several times, after I'd spent the previous minute wondering if it would be okay to ask the driver to slow down. I can't even tell you how much I'd wished that I'd spoken my mind in that situation.

Assertiveness wasn't just about learning how to express my opinions, wants and needs; it was about realising that I had a voice that was worth being heard in the first place.

The more I became assertive with the people around me, the more I came to realise that assertiveness is a great skill to have. It empowers us to explain our wants and needs without dancing around the subject, being sarcastic, saying 'yes' when we really want to say 'no', hoping someone else will read our minds or growing bitter and resentful when we think things are unfair.

I used to think it was better to people-please as much as possible because I'd appear nicer and more helpful. Many times, I was congratulated for being so agreeable and eager to go out of my way. However, at the end of the day I wasn't doing myself any favours and I felt drained – and the people closest to me were frustrated by how I put myself last when they didn't ask me to.

The first step to becoming more honest and assertive is about knowing your own wants and needs (hence why it was the first key pillar of mindful communication). After that, it's just about learning to become clearer and more honest, in a caring and respectful way. It sounds simple in theory, but we may actually be breaking a pattern that has lasted for many years. It will likely challenge you. You will probably shed a few tears. You may experience guilt and sadness and stress.

However, the rewards are incredibly valuable. More time to do things you really want to do. Higher quality relationships. Respect from other people (and for yourself!). Being less likely to feel overwhelmed and frustrated. Genuine connection with other people. The ability to say 'no' or 'yes' according to what you really want. New communication skills to use throughout your life. More fulfilment at work (you'll learn more about this in Chapter 15). Less bitterness and resentment.

But how do you become more assertive? Here are some of the things that really helped me when I first started dipping my toes in the assertiveness pool. Just by the way, I don't feel like I'm anywhere close to being an expert on assertiveness. It's taken a few years to get all the way into the pool and I can still only manage a lop-sided dog paddle. It's hard work and it probably won't happen overnight. It's a new skill and we can keep learning together.

Tips for assertiveness

1: Understand what assertiveness actually is

Assertiveness is about being able to express your thoughts, wants, needs or emotions in a clear and open way. Many definitions say that assertiveness is about confidently voicing an opinion, but I don't believe this to be true. I hardly ever feel confident when I'm being assertive! I often feel nervous, frightened and shy. But that doesn't mean I can't say what I need to say and it definitely doesn't mean that I don't deserve to be heard.

Basically, when I'm trying to be assertive, I ask myself: 'What is the clearest and calmest way I can express what I truly want (or need)?'

In Situation C on page 53, I'll share an example of assertiveness, but first I'd like to explain what assertiveness is *not* in Situations A and B.

Situation A: Aggressive

Sam woke up early on the day of his birthday and went to work. All day, he was excited to go home and be with his family and celebrate his birthday. He wondered what his wife, Rosie, had bought him as a gift – maybe tickets to the movie he'd mentioned that he'd like to go and see? He didn't really mind, though. He just wanted to relax and have a nice evening.

When he arrived home, not only had everyone forgotten his birthday, but the house was in chaos. There were toys all over the floor, the dog had dug a hole in the backyard and trailed mud through the house, there were dirty dishes all over the kitchen bench, and the couch was covered in piles of half-folded clothes.

Sam felt a sudden rush of anger. No doubt he was going to spend the rest of his birthday cleaning the house.

As soon as Rosie asked him to start packing up the toys on the floor, he told her how hopeless she was for forgetting his birthday and how she never thought about anyone except herself. He left the house, slamming the door on the way out and taking himself out for dinner on his own.

Rosie was completely taken aback by Sam's behaviour. She felt guilty and sad that she'd forgotten his birthday, but she was also hurt by his outburst. If he'd only been upfront with her, she would have apologised and they could have worked as a team to enjoy the rest of the night.

Reacting aggressively involves expressing anger, disappointment or frustration in confrontational ways. People who act aggressively might talk over other people, use intimidating body language, speak loudly and focus on their own feelings (rather than considering the feelings of others). This style of communication can be frightening or upsetting for the other person, or they may react in a defensive or aggressive way themselves.

Situation B: Passive aggressive
Let's imagine the same situation, but instead of venting out loud when Rosie asked him to pack up the toys, Sam

did as she asked, feeling bitter and frustrated. All night, he waited for the penny to drop and for anyone to remember his birthday, but no one did.

The next day, Rosie complained about how busy life was and how things were difficult to manage and Sam said, 'Well, at least *I* still remember your birthday.' He wanted to express his disappointment that his birthday had been forgotten, without directly telling her. Furthermore, he actually wanted her to feel guilty about forgetting.

Rosie did feel incredibly guilty for forgetting Sam's birthday, but she also felt frustrated. She was experiencing a particularly busy month and it was difficult just keeping up with everything. Even though she was sorry she'd forgotten his birthday, she wished Sam had just been honest and offered her a reminder.

When people react in a passive-aggressive way, they might be unwilling to voice their opinion or thoughts, hiding their true feelings, valuing themselves less than other people, isolating themselves and agreeing with others out loud, even if they don't actually agree. Meanwhile, they may harbour resentment or try to express their feelings indirectly.

Situation C: Assertive
Again, let's look at the same situation. This time, when Sam arrives home and finds the house in chaos, he says to Rosie, 'It looks like it's been a hectic day and I think you might have forgotten that it's my birthday.' Even though he still feels angry and disappointed, he can clearly and calmly articulate the truth (even showing some empathy for Rosie

by recognising what a hectic day it must have been for her). Rosie apologises and suggests that they all go out for dinner to celebrate. They do a quick tidy-up of the house and then have a nice meal together.

Assertive behaviour involves using a conversational tone, expressing thoughts and feelings while valuing the thoughts and feelings of others, maintaining open and friendly body language, being honest and approaching the conversation with tact and respect.

Being assertive can be difficult in the heat of the moment, but it is really important to identify what you actually want or need, and to find a way to express that as best as you can!

2: Learn to say no

You can say no when other people ask you for something. You can disagree with someone else's opinion. You can even say no without having to give a reason! Saying no is great for two big reasons. The first is that it means more to other people when you say yes – they'll know you're saying yes because you genuinely want to, not just because you feel obliged to. The second reason is it feels empowering, perhaps not straightaway, but later, when you're spending time doing something you actually want to do rather than doing something you don't want to do, you'll understand!

3: What you expect is usually far worse than what actually happens

When I took my overalls back, part of me was still expecting the assistant to become angry and start yelling, everyone

> would be looking at us, they wouldn't refund my money, I'd
> start crying and I'd have to avoid going back to that store
> ever again. Of course, it didn't turn out like that at all. Just
> remember that your imagination is probably expecting the
> worst, but that's rarely what the outcome will truly be.

Pillar Four: Empathy

Have you ever had someone be completely honest and assertive with you and it felt a little confronting? Well, sometimes, honesty and assertiveness can do that. We live in a society where people tend to sugar-coat things, tell white lies and boost other people up as much as possible because it makes everyone feel nicer. So when people are honest and assertive, it's not always easy to process; and vice versa – when we start being more honest and assertive, other people can find it challenging.

It can be really important to know that other people may find your honesty and assertiveness a little intimidating at first (although they may also find it refreshing and helpful!). So be gentle in your approach and be prepared for them to put their defences up. They may react emotionally, challenge what you said, ask you to clarify something, or ask if you're 'having a bad day' or if you 'woke up on the wrong side of the bed'. Allow this to unfold, without reacting in return. Tap into your own empathy and compassion, knowing that it's not always easy to hear other people's opinions and ideas.

You can also be empathetic when someone is trying to be honest and assertive with you. Try to put yourself in their position and remember how much courage it can take. It might be difficult to hear what they're saying (especially if you aren't used to hearing them being assertive), but try to give them space to talk.

Pillar Five: Give it time

If you find yourself stumbling on the road to better communication, give it some time. If you're becoming more assertive and honest and other people in your life are adjusting to it, give it some time. If you're still on the first step towards mindful communication and you're finding it challenging, give it some time. Communication is a bit like popcorn; it can take a little while to warm up and some pieces take longer to pop than others.

Don't forget there are plenty of ways to support and encourage yourself throughout the journey! Journal about your steps forward and the challenges you've been facing. Meditate so you can have quiet time and space to explore your emotions. Learn more about assertiveness by watching other people who use it well. Start to speak up when you might have stayed quiet, and offer your thoughts and ideas in small ways. Book yourself in with a psychologist so you can practise communicating in an impartial environment. Give yourself a nice reward every time you take a step towards more mindful communication.

You may also like to use some affirmations, such as:

- I am patient and persistent as I learn new communication skills.
- I am self-compassionate and seek support.
- I embrace the challenges of learning mindful communication and notice how they help me grow.

Pillar Six: What really matters?

When it comes to communication, we sometimes overlook the most important things to say. 'Did you pick up the milk on the way home?' might be the first thing we say when our partner gets home from work, rather than 'How was your day?' Maybe, 'I'm tired of hearing you talk about sport' is what pops out, when 'It's great to hear you're so excited about this' would be more meaningful for you to say (and for them to hear). A genuine 'I appreciate you' might often be replaced with an off-hand 'thanks'.

I encourage you, each day, to think about what you want to say that really, truly matters to the people in your life. Below, you'll find a few conversation starters, which might help you express how much you care.

- I think you're awesome because …
- It was really helpful when you …
- I love having you in my life because …
- Remember that time when …
- It meant a lot to me when you …
- I just want to say thank you because …

After all, communication isn't just about expressing ourselves, but also about enhancing our experiences with the people we love and care about – and also enhancing their experiences with us. By remembering what really matters, and expressing love, care and appreciation in our conversations, we can build stronger relationships and great foundations for healthy communication.

CHAPTER 5

Dealing with challenge and conflict

Some people are able to deal with conflict with ease and move forward like nothing even happened. They say what they want to say, get things out in the open, apologise and let go. I admire these people – but I am most definitely not one of them.

When I sat down to write this chapter, I immediately felt bombarded by painful memories of conflicts and challenges from my past. For many people, conflict isn't easy. It's confronting. It's hurtful. Some conflicts have shaken me so deeply to my core that even thinking about them years after they happened, I feel my body initiating a stress response: my stomach clenches, my heart rate increases and my thoughts start racing, trying to figure out what I should have done differently to deal with the conflict better. Because, if I'm being honest, I didn't know how to deal with conflict very well – and I still struggle, sometimes!

The basic format of my conflict-management routine used to look like this:

Step 1: I avoided talking about issues (and hoped they'd disappear) until they became bigger problems.

Step 2: I acted in a passive-aggressive way and hoped the other person would somehow pick up the message.

Step 3: I bottled up my feelings and thoughts, becoming more and more resentful.

Step 4: Eventually, I'd snap, feeling totally out of control and hugely emotional, and often causing damage to my relationships. Or, I'd just end the relationship so I wouldn't have to face up to the conflict and deal with things openly.

I'm sure I don't have to tell you that this type of conflict management was harmful for my relationships (and also for myself). It not only created stress and anxiety, it caused the breakdown of multiple friendships, partnerships and even family connections. My desire to avoid conflict was always my number-one priority, but it shouldn't have been! Conflict was a dirty situation in my perception, but conflict can actually be healthy, meaningful and empowering.

That's why this chapter will focus on using clear communication to resolve conflicts before they escalate and engaging in strategies which help us deal with conflict in more positive ways. The last thing I'll write before we dive into it is to please be patient with yourself on this journey. It's not an easy one to take and there will likely be a lot of learning curves. You won't always know the right thing to say and conflicts may not be predictable and simple to resolve. It might be helpful to choose at least one form of self-care now, so you can use it whenever conflicts feel overwhelming and you need some time for yourself. If you need some self-care ideas, you might like to turn to Chapter 8 for inspiration.

Clear communication and conflict

It's important to know that clear communication often reduces the need for conflict. When we can openly express our thoughts, needs, feelings and desires in calm and assertive ways, little seeds of problems don't grow into solid and inflexible trees. As Simone's story demonstrates (on page 64), using mindfulness can help us identify the real issues, communicate effectively and then move forward. Let's take another look at an example of how this could work!

Imagine you've heard that a friend said something unkind about you behind your back. The first things you might feel like doing are deleting their number, blocking them on social media and talking about them behind *their* back. Or perhaps you might take their unkind words to heart and start blaming yourself, wondering what's wrong with you and wishing you were different.

However, let's imagine that you realise this situation is calling you to step up and use some conflict-management skills. Here are some tips on what to do next.

Understand your emotions with self-compassion

Take time to process your own hurt, anger, sadness, disappointment, frustration or guilt. You may like to speak with a mental health professional, or call a helpline if you feel like it would assist you in untangling your thoughts and emotions. Create a safe space for yourself to write, meditate, cry or do whatever else might help you to connect with and process your feelings. Once the emotion has been soothed with self-compassion and understanding, you will likely be in a calmer and more rational state to deal with the conflict.

Create a post-conflict plan

If you know that resolving conflict is particularly difficult for you, and you feel worried things might not go well, be sure to create a post-conflict plan you can stick to. This may involve journaling, speaking with someone who can support you, or doing something nice for yourself – anything that will help you feel safe and cared for once the conflict has been addressed.

Find your potential for forgiveness

When we go into conflict without any spark of forgiveness, then the conflict isn't likely to be resolved in a positive way. It can be important that you at least feel a potential for forgiveness, even if you aren't ready to completely forgive the other person just yet. Remember that being forgiving isn't just for the benefit of the other person; it's for you, too. Clinging to anger, shame and hurt is more likely to harm you than them in the long term because it can create stress and relationship breakdowns.

Breathe

Take some deep breaths before, during and after conflict to help manage stress and find a sense of calm. There's nothing wrong with being nervous or experiencing stress when it comes to conflict, but breathing will help temper your nerves and decrease the likelihood that they'll interfere with your communication and intentions.

Use mindful communication skills

Be honest, assertive and open, then listen actively to the other person. Go back to the previous chapter for a refresh, if you like!

Be ready to compromise and problem-solve creatively

You may have some ideas for how to resolve the conflict, but it's important to be ready to work with the other person – you're both involved, after all! It could be helpful to picture the conflict as a puzzle; allow yourself to be motivated by the challenge of putting the pieces together and working with someone else to get it right. Ask if the other person has any ideas or opinions on how to move forward and then discuss all the options together.

Show empathy

Conflict might not be easy for you, but it might not be easy for the other person either. Let them know that you care about them and that you want to find a solution so you can strengthen your relationship and move forward.

Also remember that there are two sides to every story and it's an opportunity for you to view the situation from their perspective. You may not agree with them, but you can still express an interest in learning more and understanding their point of view.

Agree to disagree

Unfortunately, there might not always be a solution to your conflicts and the best that can be decided upon is agreeing to disagree. If you feel like the communication is going around in circles and nothing is getting resolved, it could be time to call it a day. Let the other person know that you'll have to agree to disagree for now and keep in mind that this isn't always a problem. Everyone is different – with different experiences, beliefs, values, thoughts, feelings, insights and opinions – and we're not always going to agree with each other. At this point, you'll have to decide whether you can move forward knowing that you have a difference of opinion, or whether you need to take some space and time to heal, or even end the relationship honestly.

Let's now return to the imaginary scenario of your friend saying something unkind behind your back, and explore one way it could play out if you were to use mindful conflict-management skills. Keep in mind that there are many different ways this could unfold.

You might start by acknowledging that you feel upset about the things your friend has said. Perhaps you also feel betrayed and angry. You might take a bath and leave your phone out of the room, allowing yourself to explore what your emotions feel like in that moment. There might be a big knot in your stomach and a heaviness throughout your whole body. You recognise that it's a tough situation and you self-compassionately acknowledge that it's understandable your feelings are hurt.

After a day or two, you may notice that you're feeling less upset and part of you wants to talk about it all with your friend to find out what happened from their perspective and explore how you could move forward. You may not be ready to forgive them yet, but the spark of potential forgiveness is there.

You organise a meeting with your friend at a safe and quiet place, and you decide to attend a yin yoga session afterwards as part of a post-conflict self-care plan.

Even though you might be feeling nervous, you practise some breathing techniques on your way to meet your friend, focusing on deep breathing and the point of stillness (described in Chapter 2).

When you sit down with your friend, you calmly explain that you heard about what they said behind your back, and that you feel hurt. You might also say that you would like to understand what happened from their perspective, if they want to talk about it.

As the conversation continues, you attempt to understand their point of view, showing compassion towards them for being in this difficult and possibly awkward situation. You know that's it's not always easy to be called out on mistakes and you know that your friend is also upset about hurting your feelings.

Your friend apologises and because you feel heard and understood, you decide to let it go and move forward.

After the meeting, you attend the yin yoga class and focus on being mindful and taking a break from thinking about the conflict for a while. If your friend doesn't apologise, you might be feeling upset and angry, but you go to the yin yoga class as planned and find it helps settle your emotions. This gives you the headspace to think clearly and deeply about what you want from this friendship in the long run.

Simone's story

When Simone found herself having small, silly arguments with her husband, she realised that mindfulness could be incredibly helpful. She used to feel like the Hulk when she got angry – her emotions would grow and grow as she was fuelled by other issues that weren't actually relevant to that particular argument. Now, whenever they start to have a heated conversation, she takes a moment to think about why they're arguing. Did her husband really do something wrong, or could she be blowing things out of proportion? Simone uses mindfulness more and more to help her identify the actual issues which have caused conflict, and then has a calm conversation about it with her husband so they can move forward as a team.

Moving forward after conflict

Conflict is not necessarily a sign that your relationship is wrong, toxic or doomed to fail. When I was younger, I believed that conflict was the beginning of the end; that it proved the relationship wasn't meant to be. As a result, not only did I fiercely avoid conflict, I was offended by anyone who began a conflict with me, too. No matter how it started, I perceived conflict as 'bad' and I struggled to move forward from it.

Hopefully, the first part of this chapter has given you some ideas on how to deal with conflict before and when it's occurring.

But what happens next?

What happens if the conflict has opened up wounds and you're left hurting? Or if it triggers stress, anxiety or depression? Or if you feel like using unhelpful coping mechanisms to deal with things? What happens if you're left feeling guilty, ashamed, misunderstood or invalidated?

Below, you'll find some suggestions for moving forward after conflict, but I'd really encourage you to speak with a mental health professional if you feel like you could use additional support and guidance.

Tips and techniques for moving forward after conflict

Maintain clear boundaries. After a conflict, you may need some time to process and heal. Set clear boundaries and try to let the other person know those boundaries in a gentle and tactful way. For example, 'I don't feel able to talk about this right now. Can we continue this conversation tomorrow night, after we've had some time to think about it?'

Engage in self-care. Look after yourself in meaningful ways and be sure to check out Part Three of this book for some self-care ideas.

Seek further support. If you notice that you are experiencing difficult emotions or turning towards unhelpful coping mechanisms, it can be really beneficial to seek further support. Speak to someone you can trust (who won't cause further problems between you and the person you're in conflict with), call a helpline, visit a psychologist or speak with your doctor. Often, talking about challenges can help you gain new perspectives, understand things better and find ways to move forward.

Forgive yourself. Many people feel guilty or ashamed about the role they played in a conflict. I know I tend to worry about how my words or actions have impacted the other person. I often regret things that didn't go to plan during the conflict and I go out of my way to unnecessarily 'make it up' to the other person. It can be important to remember that it's not your fault if conflict occurs, or if you don't handle it as well as you could have. You can apologise, compromise and work through conflict without talking yourself into believing that you're a bad person! It's normal to engage in conflict from time to time and to learn from those encounters so you can strengthen and develop your relationships. If you can't shake shame or guilt over a conflict, then here is a meditation which can help.

Meditation for self-compassion

Find a comfortable space to sit quietly and start becoming grounded in the present moment. You could do some mindful breathing or a short body scan, or tune into each of your senses. You may also like to close your eyes.

When you feel ready, start to observe your emotions, without judgement. Simply notice how you're feeling. For example, you may notice that you're feeling hurt, sad, guilty, stressed, angry. There may be a whole constellation of emotions.

Begin to imagine some kind words you would say to a friend if they were experiencing all your emotions. How would you comfort them? What would you say to ensure they felt loved and supported?

Now begin to direct those kind words to yourself and your emotions.

Practise speaking to yourself in a compassionate way and acknowledge all your emotions with kindness and open-mindedness. It can help to imagine yourself holding each of your emotions in your hands; gently explore each one in turn, examining what they look like and feel like.

Once you've finished compassionately exploring your emotions, bring your attention back to the room and open your eyes.

CHAPTER 6
Fostering deeper love and support

Back in the days when stress was often clouding my little world, I felt disconnected from those around me and desperate to be heard and understood. Emotionally, I tended to seesaw between anxiety and exhaustion. A few weeks could pass during which my thoughts would seem to be racing from the moment I woke up until I fell asleep at night. Even though I was rushing to keep up, I felt like I was always a few steps behind where I needed to be. As with most unsustainable things, my energy would eventually fall completely flat and I'd spend at least a few days feeling like I was on autopilot, simply getting through what I needed to with as little thought and emotion as possible.

This method of functioning had various impacts on my relationships, from blocking my opportunities to find support and acceptance, to making me into an unreliable friend. It didn't help that I also struggled to communicate my needs and instinctively shut myself off when life felt tough.

When I first started practising mindfulness, I realised several things. One, I didn't want to keep disconnecting myself from the people around me, especially when I needed support. Two, I had to learn how to clearly communicate my thoughts and feelings in open and nonconfrontational ways. Three, if I put in more effort to improve the quality of my relationships, I'd feel more connected with those people. Overall, I was excited to help myself facilitate stronger, more authentic, relationships.

I can't pretend that the process has been an easy one. It wasn't long after I started practising mindfulness that my parents separated and my own long-term relationship ended, shaking up the stability I'd relied on for so long. Suddenly, I was moving out of the home I'd lived in for the past few years, saying goodbye to people I cared about, letting go of a future I'd thought was fairly certain, while also navigating the new dynamics between my parents and redefining myself as an individual.

However, these events also created opportunities for me to shed old habits and build entirely different relationships with the people in my life. My parents seemed less like 'my parents' and I began to build new friendships with them. I focused less on maintaining the outward appearances of my relationships and, instead, felt inspired to spend time with the people I felt genuinely connected to. I started reflecting on what I wanted in my life and what I was passionate about, rather than asking for other people's opinions and just doing what they thought I should do.

It was only the beginning of my journey with mindfulness, and, over the next few years, there were four big lessons I learned about fostering deeper relationships.

Lesson one: always be open to learning more

Relationships are complicated. They can change constantly and in unexpected ways, tend to require time and effort, and may challenge you to deepen your awareness and understanding. Relationships can also encourage you to grow: to learn new things, try different approaches and tap into compassion, kindness and empathy. A long-term relationship is likely to move through difficult times and require an even deeper understanding (not just of the other person, but often of yourself, too!).

A few years ago, I started learning about relationship attachment styles, in an effort to understand more about how and why I react in particular ways.[1] There are three main attachment styles – secure, avoidant and anxious. Someone with a secure attachment style tends to feel comfortable with intimacy and expresses love via open communication. People with an avoidant attachment style might feel that relationships create a loss of independence, so they tend to minimise intimacy. Someone with an anxious attachment style might worry about their partner's ability to love them back and often becomes preoccupied with relationships.

Turns out I have an anxious attachment style, which regularly influences my relationships. Before I understood this, my reactions seemed completely irrational and unpredictable. But learning more about myself gave me the opportunity to know why certain things triggered my anxieties and allowed me to find new ways to build relationships, despite the potential challenges of my attachment style.

This knowledge also prompted me to reflect on my past relationships and how my attachment style might have affected them. While I always knew I had fears of being alone and that I acted out when I felt like I was being abandoned, there was something inherently powerful in understanding more about why I think and feel the way I do.

For example, I found it extremely difficult to feel safe and secure in relationships, particularly when previous partners were avoidant, which only tended to provoke my worries. I regularly shouldered the blame, twisting something as simple as my partner disliking my outfit to being a failure on my part and a shortcoming to be ashamed of.

Another feature of someone with an anxious attachment style is their engagement in protest behaviours, many of which I realised I'd done before. From telling my high-school boyfriend we should break up (several times) while hoping he would disagree, to deliberately not answering the phone when he called me (because he hadn't answered the phone when I called earlier), my own protest behaviours tended to confuse me and wreaked havoc across a number of my relationships.

Understanding more about why I think and act in certain ways in my relationships helps me better predict my reactions and navigate my emotions as events unfold. I can identify when I'm engaging in a protest behaviour and, sometimes, choose to take a different path which will benefit my relationship.

This is just one potential area of relationships you could learn more about. There are many, many other theories and ideas that could resonate with you and empower you with new knowledge and skills.

Activity: Head down to your local library or bookshop and find some non-fiction books that focus on relationships. Be open to learning more and identifying new ways of building stable and secure relationships.

Lesson two: communicate (and keep communicating!)

Let's explore a potential scenario of good communication. Molly arrived home after a big day at work, feeling stressed about an upcoming deadline and disappointed about the amount of tasks she hadn't completed that day. Her partner, Ron, also had a tough day at work and didn't sleep well the night before. Both of them felt emotionally drained, stressed, overwhelmed and tired, and those factors could easily have been a recipe for an argument.

However, this particular couple had been working on their communication skills and they regularly checked in with each other. When Molly asked Ron how his day was, Ron spoke about how he hadn't been sleeping well because he couldn't stop thinking about his job and the negative experiences he'd had there lately. As a result, he'd been tired at work and made some silly mistakes which he then stayed overtime to rectify. Molly empathised with Ron and allowed him to talk about his challenges, offering to help in any way she could to support him. When Ron asked Molly how her day went, she told him about her upcoming deadline and how she felt like she was never getting enough done. Ron actively listened to Molly and also showed support by offering to help.

Sometimes, effective communication is simply about creating a safe space for other people to talk, being there for them and offering support in meaningful and appropriate ways. Challenges are sure to arise throughout any relationship, but communication is an important key for navigating them together.

Let's take a closer look at how an important conversation could unfold.

Jenny is a young woman living on her own in a new city. She has just started working as a teacher and feels completely overwhelmed. Even though she arrives early and stays late after school every day, Jenny usually feels like she is behind with creating lesson plans and marking students' work. She struggles making connections with her colleagues and feels excluded and lonely. Even though she loves the idea of being a teacher and of supporting students to learn and reach their potential, she is starting to wonder if she's chosen the wrong career path.

When Jenny's sister Lisa calls her after a particularly long day, Jenny is feeling emotional and exhausted.

Conversation A

Lisa: Hi, Jenny! How are you going?

Jenny: Fine. How are you?

Lisa: I'm good. Are you sure you're okay? You sound tired.

Jenny: Yes, I'm fine, I just had a few big days at work. I'll get over it. What have you been doing? How's work?

Lisa goes on to talk about her work and the conversation ends fairly quickly. Even though Lisa knows something isn't quite right, she doesn't ask Jenny anything more about how she's feeling. Lisa hangs up, feeling even more concerned about Jenny, and Jenny feels lonelier than she did before the call.

Conversation B

Lisa: Hi, Jenny! How are you going?

Jenny: Fine. How are you?

Lisa: I'm good. Are you sure you're okay? You sound tired.

Jenny: Yes, I just had a few big days at work. I'll be fine. What have you been up to?

Lisa: Just the usual, going to work, walking the dogs and catching up with some friends. It sounds like things have been tough for you and I have plenty of time to chat. Tell me more about what's been going on?

Jenny: It's actually been a really overwhelming few weeks at my new job. I've been feeling behind with all my work and none of the other teachers seem to like me. I'm tired, I'm stressed and I'm starting to wonder if I've made a huge mistake in choosing this career path.

Lisa: That all sounds really overwhelming. Let's talk about it. First of all, can you tell me more about why you're feeling behind with all your work?

Lisa and Jenny continue to talk about how Jenny has been feeling, what her different options might be and who else she can talk to for some more support in her new work role.

When the call ends, Lisa feels glad that she could help her sister, and Jenny feels supported and connected.

Open and honest communication isn't always easy and it can take more time, an understanding of listening techniques as well as compassion and empathy; however, it can also result in a number of incredible benefits. It can help us feel more connected and supported, it allows us to hear different perspectives, it enriches our relationships and also tends to improve our communication skills for the future.

Lesson three: practise gratitude

It can be really important to teach ourselves gratitude, the attitude of noticing and appreciating good things in our lives. The practice of gratitude has truly shifted how I feel about my relationships because it has helped me to notice the positive aspects of the people I care about and the good experiences we share; it's also allowed me to show love in new ways.

However, gratitude is about so much more than just feeling thankful for the people we love and care for – it can also play a role in the stability of our relationships. In the 1980s, psychological researcher Dr John Gottman and psychologist Robert Levenson conducted a longitudinal study over nine years to determine the impact of positive and negative interactions on intimate relationships.[2] Gottman and Levenson found that as long as there were five times as many positive feelings and interactions between a husband and wife during an important conversation than negative feelings and interactions, the marriage was more likely to be stable. Negative interactions could include being critical or dismissive, using defensive body language, or eye-rolling, while positive interactions could include showing interest in your partner, empathising and apologising, finding opportunities to agree, and accepting your partner's perspectives. Another positive interaction could be to show appreciation for your partner – letting them know you're grateful to them.

Positive interactions revolving around gratitude could include identifying your loved one's strengths during a difficult conversation. For example, by saying 'I know this is a difficult conversation, but I appreciate how open and honest you are.' You could also thank them for things they've done well, or express your gratitude by being compassionate and considerate during conversations.

Furthermore, gratitude can help us balance out our natural negativity bias and the impact it can have on relationships. The negativity bias is the tendency for our brains to be more sensitive towards unpleasant things; basically, we have evolved to focus on negativity because it helps us quickly learn how to avoid danger and pain. In early human history (back when we had to regularly avoid getting eaten by predators) we largely relied on our intelligence to stay alive. Being able to quickly and easily detect threats using the negativity bias made it more likely that we would identify danger and escape.

However, this skill of quickly detecting and understanding threats has taught us to look for negative stimuli more than positive stimuli. In addition, when we receive equal amounts of negative and positive stimuli, we will naturally focus on the negative more than the positive.

In order to help me cultivate gratitude in my relationships, I do two things: I keep a gratitude jar and I talk about gratitude with my loved ones.

Gratitude jar

A few years ago, on the first day of January, I got a pen and a small piece of paper and described an experience with my partner that I was grateful for. I folded up the note and placed it in a jar. About once a week, I did the same thing – I wrote about another experience I'd had with him and put the folded-up note in the same jar.

Three-hundred and sixty-five days later, on the first day of the following new year, I opened up the jar and read over all the experiences I was grateful to have shared with my partner that year.

I learned two things from this activity. First of all, I realised how easy it was to forget my happy memories! Almost all of the things I'd written about had been forgotten and I was so glad I'd kept the reminders. Second, it was lovely to start the new year by reflecting on all the good things that had happened to my partner and me.

If you like, you could include your partner, family or friends in this activity. Once a week, you could all contribute to the gratitude jar and begin the new year by reading and sharing each other's happy memories about each other. You can also complete this activity on your own about any topic you choose. You could focus on gratitude at work, gratitude in your everyday life or gratitude for yourself and your achievements, skills or qualities.

Talking about gratitude

It can also be fun and meaningful to talk about gratitude with the people you care about. By observing and acknowledging each other's qualities, it helps us connect more and feel appreciated.

Here are some gratitude conversation prompts. (I'm going to use the word 'partner', but feel free to replace this word with friend, mum, dad, brother, sister, child or whoever else you may be talking about gratitude with.)

- Name one accomplishment your partner has achieved and why you're proud of them.
- List three features you love about your partner.
- Describe something your partner did to help you and why you appreciated it.

- List three positive qualities of your partner's personality.
- Share one reason why you admire your partner.

Lesson four: spend mindful, quality time with others

When I think about spending mindful, quality time with the people I care about, there are three main attitudes that come to mind: presence, nonjudgement and curiosity.

Presence

Focus on being present with your loved one by setting aside (or minimising) distractions, such as your phone, tasks that require concentration, and activities that create a lot of noise. It can be important to use the different elements of mindful and active listening, such as making eye contact, maintaining open body language, reflecting content and feelings, summarising and confirming, giving encouragement and showing compassion.

It's also helpful to notice if you're mentally present: are you thinking about all the tasks on your to-do list? Wondering what you should do on the weekend? Planning ahead? Or are you genuinely listening to your loved one and contributing to the conversation, bringing your attention back to the present moment whenever you notice it has wandered?

Nonjudgement

Being objective and nonjudgemental is a great way to help your loved one feel like you're taking the time to listen and understand things from their point of view. Even if you don't necessarily agree with them, try not to engage in defensive behaviour or respond with critical words because this may quickly shut down the conversation and potentially create discord.

How to practise nonjudgement in a conversation:

Remember that your actions can speak louder than your words. Try to keep an open expression and avoid eye-rolling, raising your eyebrows or shaking your head whenever your loved one is expressing new ideas or thoughts.

Be aware of 'should' and 'shouldn't'. Often when using these terms, we are expressing some kind of judgement. 'You shouldn't be doing that' or 'You should do this.' Whenever you notice a 'should' or 'shouldn't' coming up in your sentence, ask yourself if it's judgemental – and if it is, what is something more open-minded you could say instead?

Know that it's alright to ask for a moment to collect your thoughts. If your loved one has told you something that has triggered judgement, ask for some time to think about your response.

Keep the conversation focused on their perspective. Challenge yourself to learn as much about their perspective as possible so you can understand more about what's actually happening for them. Ask open-ended questions and reflect their thoughts and feelings to help them share more with you.

Let's take a look at an example of judgement and nonjudgement.

Jessica wants to share with her partner, Charlie, that she is thinking about studying photography so she can eventually quit her job as a teacher and become a full-time photographer.

As you read through Charlie's potential responses, notice which ones demonstrate judgement and nonjudgement.

Response A: 'I can see this is really important to you and I'd love to hear more about your idea.'

Response B: 'You should probably wait. You haven't been a teacher for very long and it would be good to stick it out for a while.'

Response C: 'Tell me more about this change and how you think it might work out. I'd really like to understand.'

Response D: 'You don't even have any photography skills! That's a terrible idea.'

Response E: 'You should quit right now and get rid of your awful job. You've been miserable ever since you started working there.'

As you may have guessed, responses A and C were the least judgemental, while responses B, D and E were more judgemental. Even though in Response E, Charlie was agreeing with Jessica's idea, he was expressing his own opinions without asking to hear about the situation from her side.

Curiosity

By going in to a conversation with curiosity and a readiness to learn, you will likely be perceived by your loved one as being more open-minded.

Imagine you've had an idea about redecorating a space in your home and you want to tell your friend all about it. When you start talking to your friend, they are genuinely interested in learning more, they ask questions that relate to what you've been saying and they encourage you to share as much as you would like to. This friend has shown curiosity in learning more about your idea and, by doing so, created an atmosphere where you can express yourself and feel more connected with them.

By integrating presence, nonjudgement and curiosity into conversations with our loved ones, we naturally foster mindful quality time and deeper support and connection. The people around us tend to feel more heard and understood, we gain new perceptions and learn more about our friends and family; together, our relationships grow stronger.

PART THREE

Self-care

CHAPTER 7

Making space for self-care

Have you ever heard the story about the teacher who walks into a classroom with an empty jar? He puts the glass jar down on his desk and places large rocks inside the jar until they reach the top. He asks his class if the jar is full and they say yes.

The teacher then gets a bag of smaller stones and places them inside the jar with the bigger rocks, shaking the jar so they all combine together. Again, he asks the class if the jar is full, to which they reply yes.

The teacher gets a bag of sand and pours it into the jar, filling all the gaps between the rocks and small stones. This time, the class isn't so quick to agree that the jar is full!

Finally, the teacher pours a glass of water into the jar, mixing it together with the big rocks, small stones and sand.

He asks the class, 'If this jar represents your life, what do you think it means?'

One student replies, 'It doesn't matter how many things are happening in your life, there's always room for more.'

The teacher agrees that could be one interpretation, then he goes on to share another idea. 'The large rocks represent all the big things in your life: your family, your purpose and dreams, your health and wellbeing.

The smaller stones are some of the other areas of your life which help to give it meaning: your work, friendships, money, home and hobbies. The sand and water are like everything else which fill up the rest of your time, such as vacuuming the floor, watching television, going shopping and running errands. But what would happen inside the jar if we started with sand and water?'

The water and sand (the less meaningful activities in life) would fill the jar and wouldn't allow room for anything else.

I remember the first time I read this story, everything just clicked. The truth is, we do only have so much time in a day. We need to be conscious about how we fill up our jars, so the really meaningful things can fit. One of the challenges in modern society is that sand and water activities ('filler' activities) are becoming more and more easily accessible and addictive. We can spend days binge-watching a new show on Netflix. We can go shopping online whenever we feel like it (not to mention being able to spend money we don't even have yet, thanks to credit cards and 'buy now, pay later' options). Many of us spend hours each day scrolling through social media, without even realising how much time we're using. More than ever, it is *so important* to choose how we spend our lives. Prioritising is absolutely key.

And there's one area of life which I think tends to get overlooked and under-prioritised: self-care. Self-care is more than just an activity which helps us feel good. When you look at all the most important aspects of your life – such as family, purpose, health and wellbeing – self-care is like the soil that allows all those things to grow. When we aren't taking good care of ourselves, we can be irritable and less compassionate in our relationships. If we don't take the time to understand ourselves and our needs, then how can we feel purposeful and work towards what we really want? Without self-care, our health and wellbeing can suffer in many different ways, such as experiencing higher stress levels and lower immune systems. Self-care is a fundamental, underlying aspect of all the most important things in our lives and it empowers us to become the best versions of ourselves.

There is somewhat of a misconception that self-care is lazy or selfish, so I'd like to take some time to clarify exactly what self-care is – and what it isn't.

What self-care isn't

First of all, self-care isn't so much about 'switching off' – for instance, by watching television or overindulging – but more about looking at what will genuinely nourish your needs and wellbeing. It's about curating a deeper understanding of what is good for you and then doing it, even when you might feel like you can't be bothered. For example, meditation is an activity that helps me to go inward, process my thoughts and feelings, tune in to my body and unwind. At the end of a long day, it's not always easy to take that time for myself. I might feel like I need to push myself to keep working at night after a full working day, or scroll through social media so I can look at other people rather than turn my attention towards myself. I could spend hours on the couch watching television (which is something I still often do, even though I know there are better ways I could be spending my time!). Sometimes, self-care actually takes *more* effort than many of the other things we could be doing. Which means it shouldn't be perceived as laziness! By definition, laziness is about choosing not to work or take action, even though you're physically able to do so. When you engage in self-care, you're making a choice to do it and you're following through with your commitment.

However, it is important to look at the types of self-care we engage in; are they activities that work for the greater good of our wellbeing, or are they excuses to indulge in activities that aren't actually conducive to living our best lives? While there's nothing necessarily wrong with engaging in other activities, it's often necessary to identify when an activity isn't helpful self-care so you can engage in actual self-care later.

Self-care is also not about avoidance. Several years ago, I was struggling to deal with the breakdown of some of the most important relationships in my life. I was studying a new course, but the friends I'd made over the previous three years were studying something different and I was finding myself feeling more and more lonely. My parents had separated and I was feeling disconnected from my then-boyfriend. My sister had recently moved out after living with me for the previous few months and we weren't on great terms thanks to several misunderstandings.

So I took up running because I wanted to do something healthy for myself. Every time I put on my running shoes, I felt relieved because it meant I could escape everything and be distracted by the sensations occurring in my body. I ran and ran and ran, thinking I was doing what was best for me. Even when my body ached and I knew I was pushing myself beyond my limits, I thought I was doing the right thing. It wasn't until later that I realised I wasn't really engaging in self-care – I was avoiding things I needed to deal with. I wanted to avoid interacting with the people in my life because I didn't feel as though I was on the same page as anyone else. I wanted to avoid making decisions about how to move forward. I wanted to ignore the sense of failure I felt at my inability to knit my relationships back together and, instead, revel in the success of running one more kilometre than I did the last time.

If you find yourself engaging in self-care to avoid, then perhaps the best form of self-care is actually to face whatever issues may be lingering in the background and deal with them properly. When I started noticing injuries, like regular knee pain and having such tight hips that I struggled to walk in the mornings, I realised that I couldn't keep running forever. Since then, I've intentionally reconnected with the people I care about and tried to make peace with the relationships which didn't continue to grow.

Finally, self-care isn't selfish. I used to forgo self-care because I thought it made me less hard-working, less dedicated to my dreams and less helpful towards others. At the time, it didn't make sense to me that self-care actually helped me do all those things *so much better* and that by engaging in self-care, I was doing myself (and everyone around me) an incredible service. If you ever feel guilty for engaging in self-care that allows you to be your best self, remember that it isn't selfish. You're simply helping yourself so that you can help the people around you.

What self-care is

Self-care is a responsibility. It's not always easy to recognise the best way to take care of yourself, to say no to less caring alternatives and to dedicate yourself to your own self-care. It might mean saying no to a social event because you need time to relax after a busy working week. Or self-care could involve getting out of bed earlier on the weekends so you can exercise or meditate before everyone else wakes up. Self-care might mean spending a little extra money on natural skincare (instead of the harsher alternatives) or putting in more effort to make your own meals rather than regularly buying takeaway.

Although self-care can be a wonderful solution for when you might be feeling anxious, depressed, unwell or burned out, I believe the real benefits of self-care revolve around prevention. If you can implement self-care consistently and compassionately, then it can help to protect you from various unpleasant and unnecessary physical or mental health experiences. While it may not prevent them altogether, self-care can enable you to build resilience, listen to your needs (and fulfil them), ask for support sooner and give yourself time and space to recharge, heal and move forward.

Although vital self-care might sometimes require a huge amount of willpower, there should always be a gentleness to self-care and how we implement it. Our self-care practices should take into account that we are always changing, and that what helped last time may not be as helpful this time. When things don't go how we planned, we can show ourselves self-compassion, and focus on what we learned and how we can grow, rather than ruminating on or criticising ourselves for what may have gone 'wrong'.

For example, when I had surgery for my wisdom-teeth removal, I was totally prepared for self-care. I had a number of movies to watch, plenty of delicious food I'd be able to eat and time off work to chill out on the couch and recover. In all honesty, I thought after two or three days, I'd be back to my regular self. Once a week had passed and I still felt lousy (I'd had an allergic reaction to one of the medications, wasn't eating properly and had trouble speaking as a result of some impermanent nerve damage), I started to sink into sadness. I felt isolated and frustrated. I was worried about my speech problems and how long I would take to recover. Mostly, though, I felt ashamed and powerless. Ashamed that something as simple as wisdom-teeth removal could bring me down, ashamed that I hadn't taken better care of myself, ashamed that my own expectations had resulted in disappointment. And I felt powerless being trapped with all those thoughts and having no energy to get off the couch or connect with other people who could help. I felt like such a massive failure.

During challenging times, it's really important to remember that self-care isn't about having a 'quick fix' or placing higher expectations on ourselves because of it. I learned that self-care is more about being gentle and kind towards myself and about letting go of expectations by embracing a gentler and more flexible approach towards recovery, change and healing.

On the other hand, self-care can also be about challenging ourselves to honestly reflect on what is and isn't good for us and sometimes encouraging ourselves to do things we may not be super keen to do!

About two weeks after talking with my partner and a close friend, I decided to book in with a psychologist to talk about what I was experiencing post-surgery. I initially resisted it because I really wanted to persevere with getting through it on my own, but I knew it would be good for me to talk with a nonjudgemental professional, who could offer new perspectives and support. It was by far the best decision I could have made and I still feel grateful that I chose to do something good for myself, even though I didn't particularly want to at the time.

Similarly, there are days when I don't really feel like exercising, or eating healthy food, or drinking enough water, or getting out of bed early – even though I am perfectly capable. However, I know that these are some important forms of self-care for me and that by engaging in them regularly, I can improve or maintain good health and wellbeing.

Sometimes, therefore, self-care isn't just about doing what makes us feel happiest; it's about taking a holistic look at what will support and nourish us in life and choosing to do that.

Making space for self-care

There are three simple ways I incorporate self-care into my life that help me stay consistent and dedicated to my self-care practices: creating small and daily habits, making spare time and changing my perspectives. Let's explore each one of these. As we go, select your favourite tips and see if you can implement them – starting today!

1: Create small, daily habits

I'm a firm believer that the little habits we do every day can add so much meaning and value to our lives. I used to think that going on a holiday or reaching the weekend meant I could finally enjoy myself properly, but now I try to make each day count by adding in small daily habits. At the end of the day, I take five minutes to use some natural skincare products to wash my face. I often enjoy a coffee in the morning. I love taking my dogs for walks and practising yin yoga – even if it's just for ten minutes!

I've heard some people referring to their self-care as a cup, which they fill up with self-care activities on a regular basis. By engaging in meaningful, fun, relaxing and rejuvenating activities each day, I keep my own self-care cup fairly full. It feels incredibly different from when I used to allow my self-care cup to slowly drain away while I waited for the weekend, or a holiday, or a particular event. Not only did that leave me often feeling flat and exhausted and stressed while I waited, it also put a lot of pressure on those weekends, holidays and events to go perfectly. I needed them to be extra wonderful to make up for all the time I'd spent waiting for them. However, when it comes to self-care, there's no need to wait! Keep that cup of yours feeling healthily full – overflowing even.

In the next chapter, you'll discover a range of simple self-care activities you can use as inspiration for your own daily self-care habits.

2: Let go of being busy

In a world where feeling busy can start from the moment you open your eyes in the morning until you fall into bed at night, letting go of the to-do lists often seems near impossible. It's a busy world and many of us work hard to keep up. It sometimes seems as though we don't even like to give ourselves permission to slow down and take some time off until we're totally exhausted and burned out (and even then, we might still resist!).

I used to love having a busy life. When someone asked me how I was and I said 'busy' and then started talking about all the different things I was doing, it made me feel great. Important. Hard-working. Admirable. It didn't occur to me that I was keeping myself busy and taking on more than I could handle to the detriment of my own wellbeing.

During one of the busiest years of my life, I was studying full-time, working two different jobs and volunteering. I was sick more times than

I'd ever been before. I had cold after cold, an ear infection and regular back pain. I experienced stomach issues which lead to ultrasounds and multiple trips to the doctor. I was stressed, I cried often, I didn't get enough sleep and I'd often wake up in the morning wondering how on earth I was going to get through the day ahead. I can still remember the feeling of dread in the pit of my stomach when my morning alarm went off.

When I finally did slow down and start engaging in healthy self-care, I realised that being busy wasn't worth it. I would rather study part-time, work fewer hours and be more deliberate in looking after myself. Even though I felt trapped in everything I was doing at the time, I look back now and see how many changes I could have made.

The truth is, many people are just as busy right now as I was during that year of my life. I know there are people who struggle physically, emotionally and mentally much more than I did. They might have bigger pressures, more responsibilities and higher expectations.

'Busy' is not the badge of success that modern society pretends it is. It can be a danger to our health and wellbeing – and recognising that gives you the opportunity to consciously slow down, to discover pockets of time for self-care and to say 'no' to taking on more than you can handle.

It's okay to let go of being busy. It's okay to take time for yourself. It's okay to spend the whole day doing nothing but soul-nourishing activities which help you feel calm, joyful and content. If you're not able to spend an entire day engaging in self-care, aim for what feels achievable and try to make it a priority.

3: *Make spare time*
If you find yourself always sacrificing your self-care, then you may need to deliberately create space for it – and then commit! Here are some examples.

- Rather than buying your groceries for dinner on the way home each night, you could create a weekly meal plan on the weekend. By buying all your groceries in one go you'll give yourself an extra fifteen minutes each night for self-care.
- You could start work thirty minutes earlier in order to arrive home earlier in the afternoon and have some extra time to engage with relaxing activities.
- Rather than trying to do all the jobs around the house, see if someone else can help you out (or, if you can afford it, think about hiring a cleaner to give yourself more time).
- If you find it difficult to relax at home, book in to a meditation or yoga class at a studio a few times each week.
- Use a podcast, app or YouTube video to help you practise yoga or meditation.
- Turn off your email notifications so you don't accidentally spend your time at home doing work-related activities.
- Learn to say no to social events you don't really want to attend (or social events which take up more time than they should!).

4: Change your perspective

There are so many activities we already do in our everyday lives that could become self-care practices with a few simple tweaks! Rather than rushing through these activities, see if you can slow down and engage in them more gently, kindly and mindfully.

For example, rather than drinking my morning coffee while I scroll through social media or start answering emails, I now go outside and sit on the back step. I notice the warmth of the mug in my hands and savour the aroma and flavour of the coffee. It might be a simple change, but it gives me a great opportunity to be mindful and start my day more intentionally.

Below, you'll find a list of some daily activities that could become self-care practices with a few small tweaks and changes in perspective! Experiment in your own ways to make these activities more self-caring; for example, by moving slower and more intentionally, lighting a candle, playing some nice music, or incorporating mindfulness.

Potential self-care activities

- Drink a cup of tea or coffee. Savour the taste and aroma – and put your phone away.
- Walk out to your mailbox to check the mail. Feel the solid ground underneath you as you take each step and notice how the movement subtly stretches your body.
- Take a shower. Sink into the experience of the warm water washing over you.
- Stretch. Feel the lengthening of your muscles and flexibility of your body.
- Lie down on your bed and practise gratitude for the safety, comfort and warmth of your space.
- Do the dishes while listening to some fun music. Notice the satisfaction of cleaning something!
- Brush your hair. Pay attention to the sensation of the bristles gently massaging your scalp and detangling your hair.
- Eat. Appreciate the different flavours, textures, aromas, temperatures and health benefits of your food.
- Exercise. Try to acknowledge the benefits you're giving to your body and mind and explore all the different sensations that arise in your body.
- Watch television and give yourself a soft and slow hand massage – or trade foot massages with a loved one!

CHAPTER 8

Simple self-care practices for everyday life

Now that we've explored what self-care is and how to make time for it, I thought I'd share a list of self-care practices you could incorporate into your everyday life. My advice is to pick one self-care practice to try each day this week so you can find out which ones help you relax and recharge. Create a basic schedule so you won't forget and try to include the times for each self-care practice. For example, your self-care schedule might look a little like this:

Monday: Do a social media detox (no social media all day and
   night).
Tuesday: Listen to meditation music for twenty minutes, starting
   around 9.30 pm.
Wednesday: Meditate for twenty minutes, starting
   around 9 pm.
Thursday: Read a book for one hour, starting around 7 pm.
Friday: Practise yin yoga in bed for ten minutes, starting around
   9.30 pm.

Saturday: Take the dog for a walk and play at the park for one hour, starting at 10 am (or another outdoor activity).

Sunday: Write in a journal for fifteen minutes, starting around 8.30 am.

Let's take a closer look at some self-care practices, as well as some time-saving tips for days when you feel too rushed for self-care.

Meditate

There are many different ways to meditate, but my favourite options include listening to guided meditations (such as body scans and visualisations), using breathing techniques and listening to meditation music. For ideas about meditation and breathing techniques, you can turn to the collection of techniques at the end of this book.

I've also included a simple body scan below. You could record yourself reading it out loud and then play back the recording to guide you, or ask someone else to read it to you at a slow and soothing pace. This type of mindful meditation can be great to practise because it encourages you to simply notice (rather than judge) your body and allows you to check in with how you're physically feeling. It's a fairly straightforward meditation you can do with whatever time is available to you, and many people find it to be grounding and calming. You may notice your mind wandering at times, which is perfectly normal! Gently guide your attention back to the practice and try to let go of any distracting thoughts by refocusing on your body.

Body scan

Take a moment to lie down or sit comfortably with your spine fairly straight, and close your eyes. You may like to spend some time bringing yourself into the present moment by tuning in to your senses, noticing your breath and settling yourself into the environment around you.

When you're ready, take your attention down to the tips of your toes. Allow your attention to rest there for a moment.

Move your focus to the rest of your toes, then the arches of your feet, your heels and the tops of your feet.

Notice your ankles and lower legs. See if you can feel their weight, sinking into the furniture or floor.

Bring your attention to your knees and the backs of your knees, exploring any sensations there.

Feel the strong muscles in the top parts of your leg, including your hamstrings, quadriceps and inner thighs.

Move your focus to your groin, pelvis, hips and buttocks.

Continue moving your attention further up your lower stomach, noticing your bellybutton. Observe any sensations there.

Rest your focus for a moment on your ribs and chest. You might like to explore the soft movements of these areas as they rise and fall with each breath.

Bring your attention to your right shoulder. Allow your attention to trickle down your right arm, noticing your upper arm, then your elbow, your lower arm and wrist. Explore the palm of your right hand and the back of your hand, then try to notice each finger, one by one. Your little finger, ring finger, middle finger, index finger and your thumb. You may even notice your fingernails.

Slowly, allow your attention to flow back up your right arm to your shoulder, across your chest and over to the left shoulder.

Begin to move your focus down your left arm, starting with your upper arm, then your elbow, your lower arm and wrist.

Notice the palm of your left hand and the back of your hand. Bring your attention to your left little finger, ring finger, middle finger, index finger and thumb. Try to notice each of your fingernails.

Gently allow your attention to move back up your arm and when it reaches your shoulder, feel that attention flowing over your upper back and lower back, like a wave washing over the sand.

Imagine your spine like a string of pearls and bring your attention to the bottom of the string of pearls, just at your tailbone. With each breath, move your focus slowly up your spine, taking all the time you need. When you reach the top, take a few easy, soft breaths, feeling the entirety of your back.

Invite your attention to continue moving up your neck, to the back of your head. See if you can notice the sides of your head and the top of your head. If you are lying down, you may notice the contact of your head with the floor or furniture, or maybe you can simply feel the support of your neck, holding your head up.

Move your attention to your forehead, eyebrows and temples. Notice your eyes and eyelids and explore the sensations of all the little muscles here. Feel your cheeks and nose, your upper lip, lower lip and your tongue, resting heavily in your mouth.

Notice the lower part of your jaw, the upper part of your jaw and your ears.

Take a few more easy breaths and begin to sense your body as a whole. Your entire body resting heavily, perhaps feeling a sensation of relaxation and support.

You may like to spend a few moments observing these sensations.

When you're ready, bring your attention back to the room by noticing what you can hear, taste, smell or feel. You may notice your breath by following the journey of each inhalation and exhalation. Take as much time as you like to slowly open your eyes and notice everything around you.

Well done for taking some time to complete this body scan!

> *Time-saving tip:* Try doing a body scan whenever you're a passenger in a car or on public transport. Since you're likely to be sitting with a straight spine, you'll already be in the perfect position to meditate! Simply close your eyes and spend a few minutes scanning through your body (or you can listen to a body scan via an app).

Practise yin yoga

I highly recommend going to a yin yoga class with a qualified yoga teacher so you can have the proper guidance to enter new poses, which your body may not be used to! Once you feel comfortable and confident with some poses, you can start trying them out at home. Always be careful to listen to your body and slowly release any poses that don't feel right. The aim of yin yoga is to stretch and relax, not to cause pain or push your body too hard.

I particularly enjoy holding a few yin yoga poses in bed at the end of the day to unwind and relax before sleep. I usually spend most of my day working at a computer, so I tend to focus on poses that help my back and neck to release tension, such as gentle spinal twists and child's pose.

You can also set up a relaxing space in your home and make sure you have any yoga tools that could be helpful, such as a block, bolster, blanket or cushions. You can use these tools to support your body, so you can really relax and hold the poses comfortably for longer periods of time (approximately between three and five minutes each).

As you practise, focus on taking long, deep breaths and observe any sensations of your muscles relaxing and releasing tension. Usually, a couple of minutes into each pose, I tend to feel my body letting go of resistance and tension, which means I can soften further into the pose.

Do a social media detox

Sometimes, we need to disconnect from social media in order to reconnect with ourselves. When we spend too much time scrolling through the lives of others, we miss out on the moments within our own lives. It can take some willpower to deliberately switch off your phone when you would normally be using it, but try to be self-disciplined and stick with your commitment. You can then use that time for a self-care activity or even just get a few extra things done around the house without the distraction of your phone! If you're sitting on the bus, waiting for a coffee or standing in a queue, practise being idle and simply look around and listen.

Journal

I try to write every day in one of my various journals. Sometimes, I jot down my thoughts about the day in a blank notebook, or I use a list-making journal, or I brainstorm ideas and goals. It's a brilliant method of self-reflection and an opportunity to check in with my thoughts and emotions.

You might like to return to Chapter 3 for some journaling ideas.

Time-saving tip: Use a list-style format when you write in a journal to get your thoughts and ideas down on paper faster.

Take a bath

Since I learned how to make bath bombs, taking a bath has become an even more nourishing self-care activity for me. Bath bombs are essentially little colourful balls of cornflour, bicarb soda and a little bit of oil, which dissolve and release relaxing aromas when placed in water. I love making bath bombs because the activity feels creative and productive, and I think they make baths even more enjoyable!

You can also purchase readymade bath bombs from some beauty stores, if you like.

You might find it helpful to leave your phone outside the bathroom so it won't distract you from the present moment. Then it's just a matter of enjoying the warmth of the bath and the peacefulness for a little while.

Listen to music

Music is a wonderful tool for both mindfulness and self-care. It can offer a very rich experience, with multiple layers of instruments, unexpected sounds, melodies and beats.

A simple practice I really enjoy at the end of the day is to lie down on my bed (with my legs up the wall sometimes) and to listen to meditation music for about twenty minutes. I notice that my thoughts slow down, my body relaxes and my mind naturally becomes curious about the music. It's an easy way for me to feel present in the moment, without even really trying to be there.

Time-saving tip: Keep a pair of earphones next to your bed so you won't have to go searching for them when you get a chance to listen to music in bed.

Play with a pet

Ever since I was a little girl, pets have played an important role in my life. I grew up on a farm, with many different animals. We had dogs, a horse, ponies, tame chickens, hermit crabs, sea monkeys, guinea pigs, rabbits, fish and a cat.

Growing up, I tended to be more interested in reading books and writing in journals than looking after animals, while my mum and sister usually cared for our various pets! However, when I moved to the city at eighteen years old, I felt the loss very strongly. It was strange to adapt to a new place without the presence of an animal to create a sense of home. I missed having a dog waiting for me after a long day. I missed the excitement of waiting for a chicken's eggs to hatch and holding a little, fluffy creature in my hands. I missed being able to watch the fish swimming in the pond. I even missed the sound of the rooster waking me up in the mornings – a sound that was replaced by the early-morning movements of the people in our twelve-block apartment and by the tooting of car horns.

When my partner and I first brought home our dog Moose, my life felt truly changed for the better. We had recently moved in to a place with a nice backyard and I'd spent hours researching the type of dog which would suit us the most. We drove out to meet Moose when he was about six weeks old and he was a tiny squeaking ball of warmth with big eyes. He was the runt of the litter and quite a bit smaller than his brothers and sisters, but with plenty of personality.

A few weeks later, we picked him up and brought him home. Since then, we've gone on countless walks and trips to the park, thrown a tennis ball more times than I could count, taught Moose how to swim in the river near my family home, gone to the beach together, snuggled on the couch watching movies, vacuumed a scary amount of fur off the floor and laughed – a lot. Nearly three years later, we also welcomed Moose's little half-sister, Minnie, into our family, and things became even more interesting! Double the fun, double the trouble. And I wouldn't change any of it.

Playing with a pet can be one of the simplest and most joyful forms of self-care. Throwing the ball for Minnie and Moose is such an easy thing for me to do, yet the looks on their faces and their limitless enthusiasm triggers an enormous feeling of happiness for me.

Pet therapy has been used in many different situations to help people feel more calm and less stressed. I've seen videos which show what happens when people who are experiencing incredible hardships spend time with animals – their faces light up with the joy of the exchange. I've read studies about the calming effects of stroking a pet and about how the act of caring for another creature can help reduce depression. But for me, the strongest evidence of the usefulness of pet therapy has been my own experience.

After a long day at work, or a disagreement with a loved one, or an experience with illness, spending time with a pet always helps to boost my mood, even if it's just a little bit. A cuddle on the couch with Moose or Minnie (or both!) is regularly one of my favourite parts of the day.

So, next time you're searching for some self-care time, head to the park with your dog (or go with a friend and their dog!), watch some fish in a pond, go on a horse ride, visit a wildlife sanctuary – or even volunteer at an animal shelter so you can help make a difference for the creatures who could use a little extra care themselves.

Read a book

Something I really love to do is open up a new cookbook and read over all the different recipes. I enjoy looking at the colours of the ingredients, reading about the different spice combinations, imagining new flavours and understanding more about nourishing my own body. I've read many amazing cookbooks over the years which have helped to educate me about cooking and preparing food, as well as nutrition, ethics and sustainability.

Aside from my beloved cookbooks, I'm happy to read just about anything (though I can be prone to not finishing everything I start!). Ask me what I'd like to do on the weekend and one of the first things to pop into my head is 'Chill on the couch with a cup of tea and a good book.'

When I was in primary school, I'd wake up as early as I could in the mornings before school and read until I absolutely had to start getting ready. I borrowed the biggest books in the library for my holidays and read until my head ached.

Reading has always felt like my safe, comfortable activity and it's something I like to do whenever I need to take some time for myself. It provokes my creativity and allows me to explore new worlds and ideas. It gives me a break from the chatter in my mind and the pressures of life.

Maybe there's another activity that helps you feel the same way: rock climbing, photography, knitting, making a scrapbook, archery or painting. Whatever it is, don't forget to use it as a regular form of self-care!

CHAPTER 9

Mindful self-care

There's a big difference between going through the motions of a self-care practice and mindfully engaging in a self-care practice. When I was younger, I tried to do a range of self-care activities; I took baths, I went for walks, I drank cups of tea during afternoon breaks and I went on adventures to get out of the house. However, I didn't always put in the effort to do those things mindfully. I scrolled through Instagram instead of really appreciating my cups of tea. I spent the majority of the time during my walks thinking about things I was stressed about and trying to predict, plan and problem-solve unnecessarily. I took baths while watching YouTube videos, preferring to escape the present moment instead of being part of it.

The theme running through all my self-care activities? Distraction. I wasn't actually experiencing self-care at all; I was just going through the motions. When I learned about mindfulness, I started incorporating it into my self-care activities and immediately they felt more meaningful. Time went slower when I wasn't clicking link after link in Facebook, or watching videos I wasn't even interested in! I made an effort to connect with the present moment and, in doing so, I found myself feeling more calm, nourished, relaxed and peaceful.

You might be starting to wonder how you can engage in self-care more mindfully yourself. It's not necessarily difficult, but it does take some effort and intention. As with many mindfulness practices, you may also need to exercise patience as you become used to doing things in a slightly different way. It's almost like driving an automatic car and then switching to a manual; you might technically know how to drive a manual car and you'll already be familiar with the road rules, but it will take a little bit of time before you can get used to changing gears comfortably.

How is mindful self-care different from regular self-care?

Mindful self-care incorporates three key aspects: intention, attention and nonjudgement. Below, I'm going to explain each one, and I've also included an action tip that you can implement yourself.

Intention

Many people engage in self-care by incorporating rejuvenating and relaxing practices into their lives. Their intention is often to take time for themselves and to rest in a way which helps them go back into their lives feeling fresher.

However, I believe it can be important to set more mindful intentions when it comes to self-care. It's not always enough to simply incorporate a self-care practice into your life and go through the motions in order to tick it off your to-do list.

You can be more intentional about mindfully engaging in self-care by making a few simple choices before you even get started. For example, you could remove any distracting technology from around you or go to a quieter (and perhaps more relaxing) environment. Maybe you could set an actual intention for yourself to be mindful and focused during your self-care practice. You could also choose a time when you're more likely to be able to enjoy your self-care – for example, after dinner might work better than before dinner because you'll feel less pressure to finish by a certain time.

> *Action tip:* Next time you're going to engage in self-care, try to set things up in a more intentional way by thinking about the space, time of day and how to remove potential distractions.

Attention

A key way to be more mindful during self-care is to pay attention to the different things that might be unfolding: movements of your body; various sensory information (such as aromas and tastes); sensations in your body; the colours in the world around you; or the feeling of your breath moving in and out of your body.

You might notice your mind wandering more than you would expect, but that's absolutely fine! Whenever you become aware of it, simply refocus on the present moment in any way that feels good for you (for example, by moving your focus to your breath or senses).

Imagine you're taking a bubble bath and you realise you're thinking about an upcoming project at work. You're picturing all the things that could go wrong and second-guessing your capabilities. Once you notice that your mind has wandered, you gently pull it back to the present moment by feeling the warmth of the water, noticing the brightly lit flames of the candles burning at the foot of the bath, looking at the texture of the bubbles and sensing the weightlessness of your hands as they float in the water.

> *Action tip:* When you engage in a self-care practice, challenge yourself to become curious about it – as though you're doing it for the first time. Notice everything you can about it, from the different colours, sensations and textures to the sensations in your body.

Nonjudgement

The final key aspect of mindful self-care is nonjudgement. Whenever you notice yourself judging the experience in any way, try to let go of those thoughts and refocus on the activity just as it is.

Potential judgements could be:

- This activity isn't as relaxing as it should be.
- I don't deserve self-care because I didn't get through my to-do list.
- When (some person) on Instagram took a photo of this self-care practice, it looked so much nicer than my experience.
- I don't want this self-care practice to end because it's the only time I get for myself.
- I'm not doing the self-care practice mindfully enough.

Any time you notice judgements like these, remember that they are just thoughts and they don't have to impact your experience with self-care.

Action tip: Whenever you notice a judgemental thought, simply say to your mind 'Thank you for the thought,' and move your focus back to your senses, your breath or the environment.

Once you've been implementing the three action tips relating to intention, attention and nonjudgement, you might like to try a few more strategies to help you keep developing your mindful self-care practices.

My favourite tips for mindful self-care

Set up your self-care space with relaxation aids. For example, you could light candles, play soothing music, use calming aromas (such as lavender), cover yourself with a blanket, surround yourself with natural elements (like flowers or indoor plants), wear more comfortable clothing or dim the lighting. During the self-care practice, whenever you notice your mind wandering, you can move your attention to any of these relaxation aids, or simply appreciate the atmosphere they create altogether.

Prepare for your self-care practice by getting in the right frame of mind. For example, you could do ten minutes of yin yoga to help you slow down, or use a breathing technique to ease yourself into mindfulness. You could journal about your to-do list to get it all down on paper before you begin your self-care practice. You could even re-read this chapter and remind yourself of all the ways you can practise mindfulness. Anything that helps you feel ready to begin self-care, rather than rushing into it.

Explore your different emotions without judgement, just noticing what's there. When you pay attention to the present moment during self-care, you can also notice how you're feeling emotionally. You may be experiencing a mixture of emotions: gratitude, contentment, sadness, frustration, happiness, anger, curiosity or boredom. There's no need to try to alter your emotions, just allow some space for them to be there.

Turn an everyday activity into a self-care practice. You can do this by becoming more mindful and intentional with how you approach it. For example, I used to wash my face before bed as quickly as possible and without much care for what I was doing. When I decided to do this activity in a more self-caring way, I invested in some beautiful skin-care products and took the time to really appreciate using them. I now use a soft cloth and make-up remover first, then cleanse my skin with warm water; every few days, I follow it up with an exfoliator. I gently pat my skin dry, then spray a wonderful-smelling toner on my face, followed by an aloe vera moisturiser. Even though it's just a few minutes out of my day, it's become a really meaningful and important self-care practice that also takes care of my skin.

Go out of your way to do something particularly nice for yourself. Some of my favourite things to do every now and then include going for a walk in nature, getting a massage, taking myself out for lunch at a café, attending a workshop, going to the beach or visiting my hometown. As you engage in your special self-care activity, try to use as many mindful self-care tips as you can and notice which ones help you experience the activity the most.

Connect with the people you care about and do fun things together. You can make these interactions even more meaningful by mindfully communicating and using active listening skills.

PART FOUR

Health and Wellbeing

CHAPTER 10

Simple tips for a better sleep

At 1 am, I turned my bedside light back on and picked up my book, desperate for a reprieve from my racing thoughts and the building frustration of not being able to fall asleep. Eventually, I drifted off, only to wake up thirty minutes before my morning alarm with stressful thoughts immediately flooding my mind. During the day, I felt exhausted and scattered because I wasn't getting enough sleep.

This was a common occurrence for me in my younger years. Not only did I have trouble falling (and staying) asleep, I also made poor choices when it came to my sleeping habits. I left my phone on loud, so that calls and texts would wake me up. I would often consume coffee in the late afternoon. I didn't have regular sleeping routines and would sleep in until 10 am on the weekends, then stay up late on Sunday nights and force myself out of bed early on Monday morning. Unfortunately, stories like mine aren't uncommon, with many people experiencing sleeping disorders and difficulties.

At the age of eighteen, I was diagnosed with glandular fever and spent over a week in a complete blur of exhaustion. Interestingly, as I slept and slept and slept, I woke up to the importance of getting proper sleep and I knew I had to make some changes to take better care of myself.

After gradually implementing better sleeping routines, learning simple meditations to facilitate sleep without frustration and deciding to actually value quality sleep, I now enjoy getting my rest. I really look forward to crawling into bed at the end of the day, when it used to be an activity I dreaded.

Of course, I still have various challenges when it comes to getting good sleep. I remember when my partner and I brought home our eight-week-old puppy and spent several weeks getting up multiple times each night to settle him. Every morning, when my alarm went off at 6 am to wake me for work, I struggled getting out of bed.

Late nights tend to leave me feeling hungover (even without alcohol) and unbalanced. I often feel slightly nauseous and hungry and I struggle to focus, hence why I try to avoid late nights now. I'm also not a happy napper (unlike my partner, who loves a good afternoon nap!) because I tend to wake up from them feeling unwell and groggy.

However, I've learned to love and appreciate my sleep and I genuinely believe it is one of the most important things I can do for my productivity, wellbeing, creativity, happiness and stress management.

Why is it important to value good sleep?

Studies have shown that insomnia occurs in approximately 13–33 per cent of the Australian population.[1] Sleeping pills are currently the most common form of treatment, and, while they may help individuals sleep better in the short-term, they can also reduce in effectiveness over time and have the potential to cause a number of unpleasant side effects. While medication may be necessary for some people, others might find they can improve their sleep through various natural methods. It can also be incredibly helpful to understand why sleep is important, because we can learn to value and prioritise it more.

Sleep is vital for a variety of functions, including mood regulation, memory processing, waste removal from the brain, and learning consolidation. It may seem that when we fall asleep, we 'switch off'; however, our brains are actually completing a number of complicated and essential processes to help us maintain our physical and mental health and perform at our best during waking hours.

Proper sleep can enable us to think more creatively, improve work performance, drive better, manage body weight, decrease stress, make better decisions and improve concentration.

Creating a solid sleep routine

We humans are creatures of habit and, therefore, I highly recommend implementing a regular sleep routine. Your routine should suit you and your needs, so please don't feel that you need to strictly follow someone else's formula.

I'm a morning person and I've found that I feel most nourished by going to bed early, implementing a self-care practice or two, then waking up between 6 am and 7 am.

However, I know many night owls who thrive during the dark hours and prefer to sleep in, or who catch up on sleep by taking a nap in the afternoons.

The aim is to find a routine that genuinely feels good for you and works with the necessities of your daily life (such as work, study or caring for children).

Falling asleep without frustration

One of the most challenging things for me when it came to sleeping well was the growing sense of frustration as the night dragged on and I *still wasn't sleeping*. I knew I was tired and I knew I needed to get to sleep, yet I couldn't stop my mind from going haywire as soon as the lights went out.

Some nights, I lay awake imagining all the things that could go wrong the following day (or week, or month, or year). I was literally playing out the worst-case scenarios in my mind over and over again. Other nights, I worked myself into a state by continuously checking the clock and counting down how much sleep I was likely to get. I didn't even know that I was slowly teaching my mind to behave this way – it began to recognise the time before falling asleep as an opportunity to think, plan, stress and imagine potential outcomes.

It took a little time and effort to retrain myself to relax and unwind and allow my mind to settle down before sleep, but the journey has been well worth it. Here are some of my favourite tips for gently guiding myself towards falling asleep (without frustration!).

1: Use breathing techniques

A few years ago, I hosted my first live, in-person workshop and to say I was nervous would have been a huge understatement! As an introvert with a history of highly stressful speaking presentations, I was worried I'd forget my words completely, everyone would have a terrible time and I'd regret ever agreeing to do such a thing.

I anticipated that the night before would be difficult and that I would have a hard time falling asleep (generally the last thing you want the night before an important event that requires you to be switched on and quick-thinking!).

I actually wrote down a list of all the meditations and techniques I could try in the event that my mind ran rampant and I wouldn't be able to sleep.

While I'm glad I was prepared, I didn't even end up using the list; I fell asleep before I finished doing my first body scan! When I woke up once during the night, I practised a simple breathing visualisation and went back to sleep almost straightaway.

This was the first time I properly realised the power of using mindfulness and meditation to facilitate better sleep and I've been experimenting with even more useful practices ever since!

These are the breathing techniques I use whenever I don't fall asleep within the first few minutes of turning out the light.

Breathing stairs

Imagine your breath is climbing a set of stairs. As you inhale, visualise your breath travelling up the vertical part of the stair, and as you exhale, visualise your breath travelling along the horizontal part of the stair. You can also explore what it feels like to imagine your breath is going down a set of stairs, instead of up.

You may like to experiment with the idea of climbing towards something, such as calm, relaxation, or peaceful sleep. This can be particularly useful if you're not quite feeling ready for sleep, or if you're in a state that isn't particularly conducive for good sleep (such as when you're stressed and overwhelmed).

Breathing into the body

To begin, bring your attention to your feet and inhale. As you exhale, imagine all the tension releasing from your feet, allowing them to sink into a state of relaxation.

Complete this same process throughout your whole body, moving from your feet, to your lower legs, upper legs, pelvic region and buttocks, stomach, lower back, chest, upper back, shoulders, upper arms, lower arms and wrists, hands, neck, head and face. You can move through the body quite quickly and make your way back down again, or take more time to explore each area of the body. For example, rather than sending your breath into your feet, you could begin with the toes of one foot, then the top of the foot, arch, heel and ankle.

Circular breathing

Imagine your breath is travelling around a circular shape, perhaps moving down one side of the shape as you exhale and moving up the other side of the shape as you inhale. Focus on smoothing out your breathing and reducing the pauses in between the inhalations and exhalations.

2: Do a body scan

Similar to the 'breathing into the body' practice described above, body scanning begins by bringing your attention to your toes and gradually moving your awareness through your whole body, with the aim of simply noticing different sensations, such as material on your skin, areas of tension or heaviness, or various temperatures in your body. (For more detailed body scan instructions, feel free to return to Chapter 8.)

I often like to do a body scan practice by imagining a soft piece of material making gentle, circular movements over the entirety of my body, similar to a massage. As someone who enjoys physical touch, I find the added layer of visualisation really resonates with me and helps me sink deeper into relaxation.

Another visualisation you can try is to imagine different colours throughout your body, perhaps yellow in warm areas of your body, blue in cool areas and white in neutral areas. Alternatively, with each breath, you could visualise a soft blue colour moving through your body – blue can be a representation of calm and relaxation.

3: Write in a journal

Many people find it cathartic to write down any worries or stresses in a journal before turning out the light to help them shift insistent thoughts from their minds to paper. This can also be helpful if you often find yourself remembering important things you don't want to forget come morning! Flick back to Chapter 3 for a refresher on journaling.

4: Listen to meditation music

Music is a wonderful tool to promote specific feelings and thoughts. Have you ever noticed yourself listening to a happy, bouncy and catchy song, only to find yourself feeling more cheerful? Or listened to a powerfully down-hearted song and found yourself remembering sad memories?

Music can also be used to encourage feelings of calm and relaxation, making it particularly useful when you're trying to wind down for sleep. You might like to create a playlist of soothing songs to listen to at night, or do some research to find meditation music that resonates with you.

5: Practise nonjudgement

While it's clear that sleeping well can have numerous positive impacts on our lives, I've found that taking a mindful approach towards sleep can be hugely valuable, not only because it helps to create optimal sleeping routines. When you are struggling to sleep, the practice of nonjudgement and acceptance can be extremely beneficial.

Imagine this:

You go to bed at a reasonable time, do all you can to maximise your sleep quality, then lie awake feeling more and more discouraged and frustrated the longer the night drags on. Swirling around in your mind are thoughts about how you'll never get to sleep, why you shouldn't have bothered going to bed early, how you might as well get out of bed and why this always has to happen.

Now, imagine the same situation, but without the judgemental thoughts. Instead, you notice whenever your mind is wandering and you bring it back to the moment, focusing on your breath or a body scan. Even though it may not be easy to practise and you might experience periods of frustration, you allow those feelings to pass, reminding yourself that even though you're not sleeping, you're still resting and relaxing.

I tend to find that the second scenario may not necessarily improve my sleep, but it does help me maintain a positive mindset towards getting better sleep in the future. Rather than getting out of bed the next day thinking 'That was a terrible sleep and I'm not looking forward to going back to bed tonight,' I can instead acknowledge that it was a difficult night without creating an expectation for the coming evening.

Extra tips for a good night's sleep

Apart from difficulties with falling asleep, I also found myself waking up regularly throughout the night and struggling to drift off again.

Over the last few years, a couple of habits and tools have helped me minimise restlessness, including:

- always putting my phone on silent before I go to bed
- making sure my bedroom is dark
- listening to white noise via an app to drown out other noises
- avoiding coffee after lunchtime
- investing in a comfortable mattress and pillows
- ensuring my bed is made, because people actually tend to sleep better when they climb into a made bed, rather than a messy bed!

It's been suggested to me that trying to stay awake at night can sometimes help us fall asleep quicker than if we actually try to fall asleep! Simply lying in bed with your eyes open (but not watching or reading anything) and focusing on trying to stay awake may be a helpful strategy if nothing else seems to be working for you.

Creating a bedtime routine

I've also created a regular bedtime routine, which helps me unwind and signals to my body and mind that it's almost time for sleep.

At the moment, my routine involves getting ready for bed at 8.40 pm. It takes me about twenty minutes to brush my teeth, choose my clothes for the next day, remove my makeup (if I'm wearing any), gently massage moisturiser into my skin and jump into bed.

I spend about an hour doing a few relaxation practices (such as the ones I described above) and maybe watch an episode from a television series on my laptop. I know there's lots of advice which says to avoid screens at night, but it's an activity I enjoy and, even though it might not be a perfect bedtime routine, it feels good to me. I usually notice myself feeling tired around 10 pm, at which time I turn out the light, switch on my white noise app and usually fall asleep in a couple of minutes.

There are many different activities you can do as part of your bedtime routine and I encourage you to experiment until you find out which ones resonate most with you. Perhaps you could keep a journal about your activities and experiences until you figure it out! Activities can include any of the relaxation practices I've already described, or you could try taking a warm bath (not too hot because it takes the body a long time to cool down, therefore prolonging wakefulness), talking with your partner or a family member, doing a social-media detox, drawing or mindful colouring, or reading a book (I prefer magazines or quote-books because they help me calm down more than exciting or scary novels!).

One of my mindfulness clients told me how establishing a sleep routine had helped change her sleep patterns. Claudia started reducing screen time in the evenings in order to have more time for mindful activities. She said, 'Each Sunday evening, I write a list of mindful activities to try during the week, such as taking a mindful bath.' Her efforts soon had a positive impact on her sleep quality, allowing her to fall asleep faster and wake up feeling more rested. Claudia now also enjoys using a few journaling prompts and writing for a while before going to bed. Focusing on herself and being in the moment helps her feel more calm and grounded before sleep.

Finally, try to have some fun with the journey of creating a meaningful bedtime routine. While I do think sleep is hugely important, I also believe we can enjoy learning more about ourselves – there's something refreshing about approaching personal growth with an open and curious mind to see what might unfold.

However, if you find that you've done the best you can and sleeplessness is still regularly interfering with your life, you might like to seek further support. A number of therapies have been found to be beneficial for many people with sleep disorders, including cognitive behavioural therapy, relaxation training and sleep restriction. Describe your experiences to your GP and request a referral to a sleep specialist, or you may be able to visit a sleep clinic directly.

Action tips for a better sleep

Choose one relaxing activity to try in bed tonight. Perhaps read a magazine, listen to music, do some mindful colouring or gently stretch your body. Aim to spend twenty to thirty minutes completing your chosen activity and notice if it helps you relax before sleep.

Use a breathing practice or do a body scan before you fall asleep. To choose which one you will use, simply practise each one as I've described it (the breathing stairs, breathing into the body, circular breathing and body scanning) and notice which one evokes the greatest sense of ease and relaxation.

Create your own list of 'Tips for a good night's sleep' and turn it into an actual checklist. You can then use this checklist each night until the activities become an ingrained part of your nightly routine.

CHAPTER 11

Mindful eating and conscious choices

The more I learn about nutrition and health, the more I feel inspired to make better, conscious choices and to embrace a more mindful way of eating. I've become passionate about nourishing my body and treating it with kindness and appreciation by listening to it and what it actually needs. I feel humbled by the incredible access I have to a great range of food and drinks. I also feel a deep sense of gratitude and enjoyment that I can create and cook meals for myself and my loved ones that contribute to our overall wellbeing in positive ways.

I understand, though, that it's not always easy to make healthy nutrition choices. Between dieting fads, fast food, excessive alcohol, misinformation, peer pressure, convenience and advertising, sometimes mindful eating and making conscious choices can be difficult to maintain. Of course, there are times in my life when I don't make the best choices and I find it difficult to eat well. It might be because I'm very busy at work, on holidays or at a special event, or I might be lacking motivation generally, which makes the convenience of less healthy food choices too hard to ignore. At times like these, I'm not super-strict with myself, but I remember that each day is a new chance to try again! I choose to focus on what I'm doing well rather than what I'm not, which helps me feel a sense of accomplishment and positivity.

I'm not here to inform you about nutrition because that isn't the purpose of this book. If you're interested in learning more about food and its relationship with the human body, I would highly recommend that you read some books on the subject and seek out a qualified nutrition expert who can guide and support you.

However, I would like to equip you with a few ideas about mindful eating, and share my own 'food goals' with you. I also want to talk about self-love. While we may be living at a time when there are multiple obstacles along our paths towards more mindful (and healthier) consumption, we also have greater access to incredible foods and more education than ever before. Let's make the most of it!

Conscious choices

There are many ways to make more conscious choices when it comes to what you put in your body, but I believe it all starts with how you obtain your food. I try to purchase local, organic and seasonal food when I can, in minimal packaging. A great way to do this is to buy food and drinks from farmers' markets and wholesalers.

Another great conscious choice is to make it easier for yourself to eat a more balanced diet. I like to sit down at the start of the week and plan out all my meals, so I can buy everything in one trip. Not only does this often save time and money, but when I look at my meals for the week, it becomes clear how I can better balance out my food. For example, when I first moved to Melbourne, I cooked a lot of pasta (really, a lot!) and didn't consume many vegetables. When I started planning my meals, it became easy to see which types of foods I was consuming too often and which foods I needed to include more of.

Planning meals can be quite a simple process. I like to grab my favourite cookbooks each Sunday morning, choose seven meals, write them down on my dinner planner to stick on the fridge (so I can remember what I'll be cooking), create a grocery list and go shopping. I think this is a fantastic thing to do because it helps me easily see what I'm spending on groceries each week, my nights are much more streamlined (leaving more time for meaningful activities, like self-care) and I can easily achieve better balance in my diet.

A conscious choice I feel particularly passionate about is to eat less processed foods. Having grown up on a farm, I was really lucky to experience many natural and unprocessed foods from a young age, and this way of eating became my norm. As an adult now living in the city, I cook most of my meals from scratch and experiment with making my own versions of processed foods. For example, I've made my own biscuits and muesli bars (which were actually tastier, contained less sugar and worked out cheaper than their processed counterparts), kombucha and various breakfast cereals. My go-to breakfast is porridge, cooked with rolled oats, water and milk, topped with some brown sugar. It's easy to make and doesn't contain any of the additives found in some packets of instant porridge – plus it cuts down on packaging. I add in pieces of apple and pear, spices like cinnamon and nutmeg, or some caramelised banana. You may like to experiment with this type of conscious choice – find a type of food or a meal you would normally buy pre-made and search for the recipe online to give it a try yourself!

It can also be important to choose how you use and dispose of leftover food and packaging. Do your best to recycle and re-use what you can, freeze leftover food for other meals, use older fruit in smoothies and older vegetables in soups, start your own compost pile, use jars or re-usable containers instead of single-use plastic wrapping and store everything securely so it's less likely to go off early. I know it can sometimes be difficult to do all these things (for example, I'm yet to make my own compost pile), but just choose a couple of ideas from the list and try them out. Once you feel comfortable with those, you can try another few ideas. Slowly, but surely, you'll be making more conscious choices regarding food storage and waste.

The last conscious choice I'd like to share with you is about making the decision to stop eating when you feel full. Eat slowly, chew carefully and listen to your body when it tells you it's had enough. You might feel compelled to eat everything on the plate and to snack on extra food just because it's there, but try to respect your body and how much food (and drink) it actually needs. This is a great opportunity to practise mindfulness, too! By tuning into the sensations of hunger and satisfaction (without judgement), you can be more mindful while also creating more awareness of your body and its needs.

Mindful eating

There are so many potential ways to consume more mindfully. Over the next few pages, you'll find a list of my favourite mindful eating tips, but first I thought I'd share an example of what mindful eating can feel like.

> You pick an apple from the fruit bowl and wash it under some water, noticing the smooth skin and the cool water running over your hands. While it is still covered in water droplets, you take a bite of the apple and taste an explosion of sweetness. It is both refreshing and cooling and the aroma of the apple grabs your attention. You also notice the crunchy, uneven texture of each piece of apple in your mouth and the mixture of water and apple juice on your lips. You look at the fruit just before you take each bite, seeing the colours – red and green on the outside and creamy white on the inside. You hear the juicy sound of the apple being crushed between

your teeth and pay attention to the feeling of chewing, being careful not to swallow any large pieces.

Even though your mind might wander at times (which is normal during any mindfulness practice), you notice many different things about the apple as you eat it. The colour, texture, sounds, flavour, aroma and sensations.

You can try this same practice with any type of food. The aim is simply to notice as many different aspects about the experience as you can, without placing any judgements on it (such as 'I shouldn't be eating this' or 'This food tastes bad').

Mindful eating can be a wonderful daily mindfulness practice because it creates a richer and more meaningful eating experience, while helping us tap into the benefits of mindfulness. For example, rather than eating lunch while answering emails at your work desk, you could take a break and eat your lunch more mindfully. This could give you a chance to take a break from feeling stressed and overwhelmed; you will hopefully experience some moments of calm which will help you go back to work feeling refreshed and more focused.

Now, let's explore some specific tips for mindful eating!

Mindful eating tips

Minimise distractions

Have you ever eaten a meal while scrolling through social media on your phone? Or at the same time as you're watching television? Or when you're multi-tasking?

I'll be the first to put my hand up and say that I've done all these things (and still do them from time to time). However, I try to eat the majority of my meals without distractions so I can help myself create mindful eating experiences. I've noticed that it's much more difficult to enjoy the flavours, textures and aromas of food when I'm engrossed in a television show, or answering emails, or posting a photo on Instagram.

As you sit down to eat your meal, simply put in the effort to minimise distractions by turning technology off and trying not to multi-task; instead, just pay attention to your food.

Consume foods that contain a variety of flavours and textures

Food is often more captivating when it includes a mixture of flavours and textures. Throw together a salad with spinach, cherry tomatoes, olives, avocado and balsamic vinegar – then notice how soft the avocado feels in your mouth compared to the burst of a sweet tomato. Make a soup with a variety of leftover vegetables and spices, and just before serving throw in a handful of homemade croutons for an exciting crunch. You could try one of the meals my mum used to make when I was little (which we always got excited about). We called it a 'platter', and it was basically a plate filled with whatever my mum had on hand: nuts, leftover rice, olives, chopped carrot, peas, or any fresh herbs and vegies that happened to be growing in the vegetable garden. It was a fun way to eat a variety of different foods, while consuming a range of vitamins and minerals.

This tip is all about capturing your attention and, therefore, helping you eat more mindfully!

Go out to a café or restaurant

I personally love eating breakfast at a lovely café. The whole process brings me into the present moment and helps me appreciate my food (especially the fact that it's usually delicious and I didn't have to do anything to make it!). I order my coffee, browse through the menu, choose the option I'm most in the mood for, then just enjoy the meal when it arrives.

Sit at the kitchen table and use a knife and fork

If you really find it difficult to turn off technology during a meal, try sitting at the kitchen table (or somewhere you can't see the television). Also, if you make meals that require a knife and fork, then it's much more challenging to hold your phone and scroll through social media while you eat! This tip is particularly useful if you feel stuck in habits that involve using technology during meals.

Cook mindfully

When I began incorporating mindfulness into everyday activities like cooking, I began to see the rich experiences that were waiting for me. Vibrant colours and interesting textures, different sensations and new flavours. Creative recipes and the opportunity to experiment. Feelings of accomplishment, curiosity, gratitude and pride.

All of this was useful when, in January 2017, I received a message from Christina, a lovely woman who had been listening to my podcast; she asked me for some tips on how to prepare a delicious and nourishing meal while being present and open to the moment. She felt that cooking was an activity she tended to rush through and she wished she could enjoy it more.

Christina's question struck a chord with me, because I could still remember when I didn't see the value in any part of cooking, except for having a meal at the end. I used to try to quickly prepare a meal, feeling annoyed at the inconvenience of it all.

So I put all my thoughts and experiences of mindful cooking together, sharing them with Christina (and later, on an episode of my podcast), encouraging her to try a few mindful cooking tips.

A few days later, on a beautiful, sunny morning, I opened Instagram and found a thoughtful message waiting for me. Christina had sent me a photo of some fresh and colourful vegetables with a few words about her mindful cooking experience. She wrote about being excited to chop the vegetables and how she had noticed all the little things she might normally miss, like the aromas and sensations. Even in this simple activity, she said, she'd found a new level of cooking that was mindful, fun and more rewarding. I felt a rush of excitement about what she'd achieved.

Some tips for cooking mindfully include:

- Try new recipes that help you go outside your comfort zone and open you up to new experiences.
- Notice different temperatures, such as the coldness of your fridge, the warmth of water or the heat emanating from the oven.
- Pay attention to the different cooking motions, such as chopping, stirring and lifting.
- Check in with your senses regularly, particularly taste and smell.

My food goals

I know it can sometimes be difficult to feel inspired about healthy and mindful eating. Making conscious choices might feel overwhelming, especially on top of everything else you have to do. Whenever I'm struggling to find the motivation, I remember my food goals and the reasons why I want to put in the effort. Even though I feel like there's a long way to go before I reach my food goals, they still inspire me and give me fresh ideas.

My food goals look like this.

When I'm living at a more permanent place (for instance, in a house with a garden instead of in a rented apartment), I will create my own vegetable garden with pumpkins, tomatoes, zucchinis, potatoes, carrots and sugar snap peas. I'll also grow my own fruits:

apples, berries, pears, lemons, watermelon and rockmelon. And I'll have a little herb garden, too! I'll freeze a lot of things so I can make fresh smoothies, even when my favourite fruits aren't in season.

It would be great to have few a chickens to lay eggs and a pantry filled with preserved fruit and vegetables (just like my mum has!).

I'll have a healthy compost heap and I'll feed plenty of leftover scraps to the chickens, too.

Ideally, I'll be making my own muesli, bread, kombucha and pasta.

And I'll have an open-plan kitchen, so I can do a lot of cooking and still feel connected with people in the rest of the house.

I feel as though I'm always working towards a more natural way of obtaining food, so I can eat in a simpler way (with less sugar and processed foods) and continue learning about how to eat sustainably.

So another of my food goals is to keep finding new ways to be mindful and to make conscious choices when it comes to food and drinks, so I can improve my own health and wellbeing, and reduce my impact on the environment.

Action tip: What are your ideal goals when it comes to nourishing your body and making conscious choices? Write them down – and be as specific as you can. It can also help to identify the small steps that you can start taking today that will bring you closer to your food goals.

Self-love and respect for our bodies

When it comes to the idea of self-love and respecting my body, I can't help thinking about food. Over the years, I've tried to use food in various ways to change how I look, from losing weight to getting rid of my acne. While there's nothing inherently wrong with using food and nutrition to maintain a healthy weight and skin, I unfortunately went about it in a way that didn't revolve around self-love and respect.

When I hit puberty, I quickly gained weight and my skin broke out in painful acne. My body felt out of control and I started using food to punish myself for the way I looked. I tried to avoid eating when I was hungry, I felt angry with myself when I found a new pimple (and frustrated when this was after eating foods that would supposedly clear my skin) and I made myself feel ashamed after eating 'treats'. I remember crying as I stood on the bathroom scales to find that, despite the deprivation I'd tried to implement, I'd actually gained weight. My story is just one of many, and some people face much bigger challenges when it comes to food. And while I'm certainly not saying that self-love is a magical cure for anyone who faces difficulties with food or eating disorders, it was, in my experience, a meaningful step towards creating a better relationship with food and my own body.

Self-love is not always an easy task for people and it's an incredibly individual experience. I can't tell you how to completely love and appreciate your body, even though I wish I could! I've read books about it, I've used affirmations, I've journaled, I've spoken with various mental health professionals about confidence and self-esteem, I've analysed research, I've used a range of psychological techniques … and I still don't feel like I've discovered the secret to unconditional self-love and self-compassion!

What I've concluded is that self-love is not simply a switch we can flick on whenever we choose; it's an ever-evolving journey that feels easy sometimes, but may also feel incredibly challenging. Some days I can look in the mirror and feel great about the person looking back at me. Some days, I cringe as the flaws seem to pop out like great big neon signs. On the days when I'm not feeling particularly self-loving, I try to use kind self-talk and remember that I'm not a perfectly edited image of a woman in a magazine with great lighting, professional makeup and beautifully styled hair. I am flawed, yet at the same time I'm happy with all that I am.

Make it your mission to treat yourself kindly, to respect all that your body does, and it's likely you'll find that self-love gradually starts to flow from there. If you would like to try a self-loving meditation, I've included one below.

Meditation for self-love

Find somewhere quiet to sit, and spend a little bit of time getting comfortable. When you feel ready, close your eyes.

Begin to bring your attention into the present moment by noticing:

- the connection between your body and the floor
- the sounds in the room around you, and further away
- any tastes or aromas
- areas of tension and relaxation in your body, plus areas of warmth and coolness
- how you're feeling emotionally.

Once you feel more grounded and connected with the present moment, do a gentle scan through your body, noticing each body part from the top of your head all the way down to the tips of your toes.

Now allow a kind and positive thought about yourself to float into your awareness. It may take a little bit of time and you may notice a variety of different thoughts before you settle on one that resonates.

A few examples might be:

- I appreciate my individuality.
- I love the person I am.
- I embrace myself and everything that makes me who I am.
- I admire both my strengths and my weaknesses.
- I am proud of myself.

Once you have a kind and positive thought in your mind, try to immerse yourself in the meaning of it. For example, explore what it feels like to be proud of yourself. Notice where you can feel that emotion in your body. It might help to bring to mind someone else you're proud of and transfer your affection for them towards yourself.

You may feel challenged during this meditation, and that's perfectly okay! Let go of any unnecessary thoughts and refocus on either your positive thought, or take a break by noticing your breath.

When you feel ready, you can bring your attention back to the room, noticing all your senses and how you feel.

Throughout your life, there is one person who can always be there to guide, support and love you – and that person is you. Compassion and self-love are so important to learn about and practise because, at the end of the day, you can have a challenging and stressful relationship with yourself or you can nurture and strengthen this relationship. It's up to you which one you choose.

CHAPTER 12

Moving your body

An active lifestyle can be so much more than just obligatory exercise and boring routines. You don't need to put on your trainers at six in the morning and head out into the cold for a jog (if you don't want to!). You don't have to swim a hundred laps of the pool if it's one of the most mundane activities you can imagine yourself doing. You don't have to go to the gym and take part in classes that make you feel overly uncomfortable and uninspired. On the other hand, maybe an early-morning run fires you up like nothing else, or a hundred laps of the pool help you feel energised, calm and happy. Perhaps a class at the gym is a great way for you to exercise, while also meeting new people and enjoying the energy of working out in a group.

For me, exercise is all about experimentation. It's learning more about my body and what it needs at different times, as well as finding ways to get moving that feel genuinely fun and meaningful. An active lifestyle allows me to explore new activities and reap the benefits of exercise (without feeling like I'm going through the same old motions again and again and again).

And it gives me an incredible opportunity to practise mindfulness.

Let's rewind to early 2011, when I first moved to Melbourne. Having spent the previous fifteen or so years dancing (and absolutely loving it!), I began searching for a new dance studio. It's easy to describe what I loved about dancing: the connection with the music, how nothing else seemed to matter while I was absorbed in the movements, the elation of creating choreography from nothing. When the show *So You Think You Can Dance* began airing on Australian television, I recorded every episode and watched my favourite dances until I knew them by heart.

Even though I was shy and introverted – struggling to speak up in groups of more than two people and shaking the whole way through any kind of speaking presentation – I absolutely *loved* performing. I competed multiple times throughout my childhood and teenage years, and for someone who couldn't stand not having everything planned out, I revelled in the thrill of going out onto the dance floor for an improvised-dance competition, not knowing which song was going to play or what moves I'd make.

Once I joined a dance studio in Melbourne, I promptly fell out of love with dancing. I missed the people I used to dance with and the teacher who inspired me. I felt awkward and lonely. For an activity that had felt natural for so long, it quickly became something foreign to me, and remembering the steps felt like trying to hold on to water with my bare hands.

I stuck it out for several months, hoping to find that spark I knew had to be inside me, somewhere. But it just never felt the same.

When I started to dread going to class and spent weeks avoiding it (feeling incredibly guilty as the membership money came out of my account each fortnight), I decided it was time to let it rest for a while.

I missed the physical activity and decided to join a nearby gym. I attended boxing classes, weight-lifting classes, yoga classes and Zumba classes. I swam in the pool and ran on the treadmill. I realised that I didn't have to stick to one activity; I could mix things up as much as I wanted.

And from realising that I had the freedom to move my body in whichever ways felt right at the time, I quickly fell back into an active lifestyle. When I grew bored with the gym, I took up long-distance running around my neighbourhood. Then I started going to boxing classes and went to the local pool to swim laps. My partner and I moved to a new area and I joined the local yoga studio.

If you haven't already guessed, variety is the spice of my active lifestyle. Without it, I grow bored and frustrated and end up feeling as though exercise is a chore, rather than an opportunity to have fun and engage with my body in a mindful way.

But maybe you prefer your routine and there are activities you genuinely enjoy, day in and day out, and that's okay, too! It's important to understand what works well for you and to know that you can change things up whenever you need.

Maybe you could organise a hiking trip, or go rock climbing with some friends. Or you could try out a karate class or practise tai chi. You could volunteer to walk a friend's dog, ride a bike to your local café (rather than drive) or learn how to surf. You can find small ways to incorporate activities into your everyday life, like taking the stairs instead of the lift, or organise regular adventures to try new things.

Mindfulness and moving your body

You may already know about the various benefits of exercise: the release of endorphins, better sleep, protection from chronic diseases (such as heart disease and type 2 diabetes), the maintenance of strong bones and muscles, weight management, improved brain health and increased energy. However, an interesting benefit I've discovered over the last few years is the opportunity I have to practise mindfulness every time I move my body. It's a chance to really connect with myself and to actually experience exercise in a way that is meaningful, fun and enriching.

I can find joy in a sweaty session on the bike, when my legs are burning and my heart feels like it's racing wildly enough to shoot out of my chest. I can also find joy in a yoga pose that has me lying on the floor with my eyes closed. All experiences of exercise can present something unique, something powerful, something deeply grounding. Sometimes, we don't even need to practise mindfulness intentionally; the experience is simply so captivating that there's no room for anything but total presence.

For example, imagine you're rock climbing indoors on a challenging wall. You can feel the strength in your arms as they anchor you in place, you notice the texture of the rocky handles under your fingers and you experience each breath, using it to help channel your focus and stay calm. Every time you move further up the wall, you feel the power of your legs propelling you upwards. You may even notice different emotions as they arise – fear, intimidation, determination, excitement, happiness and pride.

You might notice a similar connection with the present moment, free of judgements and distractions, via many different exercise experiences. I now search for and savour moments like these and that's why exercise has become so much more than a chore or a simple requirement to maintain my health.

Let's explore the connection between mindfulness and exercise a little deeper, looking at the breath, bodily sensations, the environment and letting go of judgements. I hope this chapter will not only help you find more mindfulness via exercise, but also inspire you to connect more with your own body and physical experiences.

Exercise and your breath

When you're exercising, it's totally normal for your breathing rate to increase as your body works to provide extra oxygen to your muscles and eliminate more carbon dioxide. With this change comes a powerful chance to tune in to your breath.

While breathing is perhaps my most-used mindfulness technique, it's one which can easily be overlooked. On average, we breathe around twenty thousand times every single day, or approximately twelve breath cycles every minute. Cultivating awareness of the breath can take effort, but it's a practice which can easily be built over time because there are so many opportunities to try it.

Have you ever gone for a run and found yourself paying close attention to the increased depth of each inhale? It might seem like the only thing that's truly important in that moment is obtaining as much air as possible. Or maybe you've found yourself swimming laps at the pool with your focus deeply entrenched in breathing at exactly the right moments to avoid a mouthful of water.

These are just a few examples of how the breath can gently direct our attention to the moment during exercise, but I highly encourage you to try this for yourself.

Next time you're exercising, see if you can explore a few different aspects of breathing, including where you can feel your breath, how it changes and whether there are any patterns you can find. We'll explore all three of these aspects of breathing below.

Feeling your breath

Maybe you can follow each breath as it enters your nostrils, moves down your throat and fills your lungs (and then follow the journey back out again). I find this is a simple mindful breathing technique to use when I'm doing light exercise, such as walking, yin yoga and stand-up paddle boarding, because each breath cycle is quite long and gives me enough time to actually feel the different areas.

When the type of exercise becomes more intense and my breathing rate increases, I like to hone my focus to just one area of my body where I can feel my breath. Usually this area is my chest, but feel free to experiment with different areas to find what works best for you.

How the breath changes

Become curious about the changes in your breathing cycles as you exercise. You may find that everything is quite slow and calm at the beginning, then speeds up and slows back down again.

Recognise the incredible intuition of your body and how it knows to increase your oxygen intake, without you consciously telling it to. There are so many amazing ways that our bodies work and I think it's important to appreciate just how phenomenal they really are. At a time when there is so much focus on the outward appearance of our bodies, there has also been a rise in displeasure and frustration with what our bodies look like (rather than what they do).

Learning to notice and appreciate the breath is a wonderful starting point for anyone who might like to build a greater sense of worth around their body and the functions that it's actually capable of.

Breathing patterns

Another exciting feature of the breath is that it is entirely your own. In 2013, a study led by Professor Renato Zenobi of the Swiss Federal Institute of Technology in Zurich suggested that each person's exhaled breath is as unique as a fingerprint. Not only does the breath seem to vary between individuals, but it also changes throughout the day depending on chemical changes within the body.[1]

With this in mind, what can you notice about your own breath? Even though you may not be able to detect chemical compounds in your breath, there may be other individual aspects you can discover and pay attention to. Do you pause at the end of each exhale? Do you naturally breathe in time with the movements of your exercise? For example, when you run, do you inhale for a certain number of steps and exhale for a certain number of steps?

Exercise and bodily sensations

If there's one thing exercise isn't short on, it's physical sensations. I can't remember a time when I exercised without noticing something about how my body felt (and that includes all the years of exercise I did before I learned about mindfulness!). Whether it was an area of tension in my body, the feeling of my skin heating up, the releasing and lengthening of my muscles, or the sensations of my posture, physical aspects of exercise were always incredibly salient to me.

Before I learned about mindfulness, however, this was actually an area of frustration. I was constantly wanting to push past my limits (feeling disappointed when I couldn't), while I perceived the physical signs of needing to slow down or go easier on myself as problems to overcome. I always wanted to run faster and further, to achieve difficult yoga poses quickly, to swim fifty laps when I felt tired after five and to lift weights I wasn't ready for. In many ways, exercise often felt like punishment and provided a reason to feel frustrated and angry with myself.

These days, I do my best to respect my limits and to move forward at a pace that genuinely feels good for me. I can do this by mindfully tuning in to my body and understanding when I've had enough and by noticing when I'm starting to feel frustrated. Instead of being pushed by that frustration into doing exercise that doesn't feel good (and actually has the potential to cause harm), I recognise that I'm feeling frustrated and I pause to take a few deep breaths. During this time, I usually notice that it's time to slow down and show some self-compassion.

I can return to the exercise and simply embrace where I'm at, without needing to push myself more or achieve something I'm not ready for. The mindful experience of exercise is rich and meaningful enough, just as it is.

Here are a few simple steps you can take to invite mindfulness into the experience of bodily sensations. These steps also spell the word FEELS, making it easy to remember when you're exercising!

Feel

Notice what your exercise actually feels like. Can you feel your muscles supporting you, or lengthening, or strengthening? Can you feel your breath moving in and out of your body a little faster? Can you feel the different movements of your arms or legs?

Extend

Extend yourself to the point where you feel comfortably pushed, if you would like to. Exercise can be a wonderful opportunity to build your resilience and strengthen your body, but don't forget to support yourself with kind self-talk and encouragement. Notice if your inner dialogue becomes mean or critical and see if you can replace those thoughts with meaningful affirmations, such as 'I am doing really well. I'm here, I'm trying and that's awesome.'

Embrace

It can also be important to embrace the stage you're actually at with your exercise. It may not be where you want to be, your progress may be slower than you anticipated, you may achieve things quickly and then take a few steps back, or you may reach a point and feel happy just maintaining it. Try not to compare yourself to others and focus instead on your own journey and the benefits it's given you. For example, I may not be particularly flexible, but yoga gives me the opportunity to slow down, connect with my breath, tune in to my body and stretch out areas of tension.

Listen

Consciously choose to listen to your body and what it needs as you exercise. Do you need more water, a short break, a gentle stretch, a few deep breaths? Maybe the endorphins are kicking in and you're feeling energised and ready to kick things up a level? Also, be conscious of when you've had enough, even if it's earlier than you intended. Listen to your body and allow it to guide you through your experiences with exercise.

Start

Now that you know some simple tips for being mindful of your body and engaging in exercise in a self-compassionate way, it's time to get started! Sometimes, one of the hardest moments is finding the motivation to begin. I've found that the best ways for me to exercise regularly include mixing up my routine; some days, I'll go for a walk, some days I'll go to the pool and some days I'll roll my mat out and practise yoga on the lounge-room floor. As soon as I have the thought 'Now would be a good chance to do some exercise!', I try to just get started, without procrastinating or looking for excuses. Even if it's only for ten minutes, that's still better than nothing at all!

Exercise and the environment

Exercising in nature offers so many opportunities to be mindful, from the igniting of our senses to the little challenges we can discover and embrace, such as rolling hills, moving water, different temperatures, higher altitudes, abrupt weather changes and heavy rain. Nature can be unexpected, and therefore tends to draw us into the moment in a very compelling way!

There are no fancy techniques or top tips here; I simply encourage you to exercise outside and explore whatever may be there to be explored. You might have an experience like this one:

You are standing on a paddle board in the middle of a smooth, still lake. Each time your paddle dips into the water, it makes a quiet splash and then sends out waves of ripples as it cuts through the water like soft cheese. You feel the sunshine on your skin, droplets of water on your legs and your body moving intuitively to stay balanced.

Try going for a hike and feeling the strength of your legs as you climb. Go to a lake and walk around it, watching birds floating on top of the water and creating ripples. Practise yoga outside on the grass, instead of in a studio. Head down to a beach and swim or bodysurf in the salty water. There are so many ways you can blend exercise, nature and mindfulness together for a rich experience.

Exercise and letting go of judgements

Judgements can suck a whole lot of joy away from our experiences of exercise. I know that when I'm being overly critical towards myself – noticing every flaw, demanding that I change things I can't even control, or adamantly repeating negative thoughts – it's much more difficult to be mindful and appreciate the moment.

Letting go of judgements can be such an empowering thing to do and allows us to not only increase our potential for mindfulness, but helps us become kinder and more compassionate towards ourselves.

The first step towards letting go of judgements is simply noticing their presence. For example, 'I just noticed myself having the thought that I'm not good enough at this' or 'Hey, that judgemental thought about being too slow/weak/fit just came into my mind again.' Know that it's okay to have a judgemental thought – and try not to add another layer of judgement to the situation by feeling guilty about it! I used to do this all the time when I first started. Now I try to just observe the judgemental thought, as though I'm digging in the garden and I've found an unexpected worm in a handful of dirt. It's allowed to be there, there's nothing wrong with it and it's just a normal part of life.

Notice the judgemental thought, remember that it's okay to have that thought, then simply refocus on what you're doing. You could move your attention back to your breath, your physical experiences, or the environment around you.

Another helpful technique can be to simply say 'Thanks, mind!' to remind yourself that your mind may be trying to help you, but it's not always right. I first learned this technique from a book called *The Happiness Trap* by Dr Russ Harris,[2] and it's one I've used again and again over the years to remember that even though my mind always thinks it's right, sometimes it's not. For a long time, I let my own mind dictate so many of my actions unnecessarily with thoughts like 'I don't belong in a gym, I need to exercise somewhere private' or 'It's a sign of weakness to slow down before I get to the end' or 'Everyone here is better than I am and there's no point even trying.'

To show you the potential influence of my own judgemental thoughts, here's an example. When I was growing up I felt sick at the thought of swimming carnivals. Swimming wasn't a sport that felt natural to me and I talked myself into truly dreading it. In my journal, I wrote about how much embarrassment I would feel about coming last, about how people would be laughing at me and about all the mistakes I was bound to make. The one exception to this was breaststroke. I loved that style of swimming and often did quite well in those races (a sign to me that I was 'good' at it).

Once I reached high school, the swimming races we participated in were optional. I always chose to compete in the breaststroke races, while telling myself that the other races weren't worth my time because I wouldn't do well and there was a chance I'd embarrass myself.

However, in Year 11 I was elected as the leader for my sports team. My school had always been divided into three teams for the sports events (swimming and athletics) and we could win points for our teams. Coming first, second or third earned larger amounts of points, but just participating in each event also earned a point.

Once I realised how important each point was (and how little my ego mattered), I decided to sign up for every possible race in the swimming carnival. Not just breaststroke, but also freestyle, backstroke, relays – even the longer freestyle event that involved swimming multiple laps (which I came last in, by the way!). I told the team that I was entering all the races, even though I wasn't a confident swimmer and I knew I wouldn't win. And I encouraged them to do the same.

I let go of my previous judgemental thoughts and replaced them with new ones: it was worthwhile to compete in all the races to earn the points and encourage my team. I could come last and show my team that it wasn't the worst thing in the world. It was more important to me that I tried and came last than if I didn't try at all.

It was easily my favourite swimming carnival out of all the years I'd been attending them. I was exhausted, but I also felt incredibly empowered by putting my judgemental thoughts in the back seat while I encouraged myself and allowed myself to be proud of what I'd done. I found joy in that – and it was one of the first times I remember showing myself that I didn't have to believe my own negative and judgemental thoughts about not being good enough at exercise.

PART FIVE

Work, Stress and Assertiveness

CHAPTER 13

Mindful commuting and a positive start to the working day

The commute

This was how my mornings used to look.

Drive to the station. Get on the 6.12 am train and hopefully find a seat. Exactly thirty minutes later, change trains. Stay on the second train for ten minutes. Leave the train as quickly as possible and cross the railway tracks without getting stuck waiting for the train going in the opposite direction. Walk 1 kilometre (exactly) as fast as possible. Arrive at work by 7 am.

This was my morning commute for several years (except for the days when I was lucky enough to catch a lift!). While it was the same commute nearly every day, I can recall having two very different attitudes about it.

Attitude one

I wake up in the morning and already feel a tiny niggle of dread about the commute. It's usually cold, too crowded and a fairly long trip. I put on my makeup and brush my hair, picturing myself standing on the platform and waiting for the train. I imagine myself looking around for a seat, hoping I can find one. I haven't even left the house yet, but I'm already worrying about the possibility of not getting a seat on the train!

A few minutes later, I'm on my way to the station and notice myself worrying about whether or not I'll get a seat (again).

If I get stuck at both red lights on the way to the station, it means I'll still catch the train but I probably won't have time to walk all the way to my favourite carriage (the first one, because it means I'll have a shorter walk to catch the second train). I think something along the lines of 'I should have left home earlier – I'm an idiot.'

If the train is also late (which it often is), then I would have time to walk to my favourite carriage, but I might miss the connecting train later on. I take a moment to worry about that and feel frustrated by the fact that I can't control the trains.

Are you starting to see the pattern of worrying, frustration and negative thinking?

The train arrives and I see a couple of seats available, but they're window seats, meaning I have to squeeze past the people sitting in the aisle to get there. I choose my seat, make my way there and hope the people in the aisle seats are awake and notice me so I can squeeze by with minimal fuss. Sometimes, I accidentally knock someone with my bag, mumble an apology and feel annoyed by the whole situation.

Once I have settled into my seat, I close my eyes and start thinking about the day ahead. 'Did I respond to that email yesterday? What's on my to-do list? Oh, remember that phone call I don't want to make? Remember that spreadsheet I need to finish? Why didn't I do those yesterday? I can't forget to book those flights and accommodation – better not make any mistakes!'

Suddenly, I'm at the next station, changing trains and feeling stressed.

The next train ride is over too quickly, because once I felt stressed, I want to just stay longer on the train.

There are a few potential problems when it comes to walking to work. If it's raining, my feet and socks get wet. If it's Wednesday, the streets are narrower than usual because the bins are out for collection. I don't particularly like having to navigate the bin situation to overtake the slow walkers! I also don't really like people walking too close behind me. I don't like waiting for cars while I cross the side-streets. I definitely don't like missing the green walking light at the main road and having to wait a few extra minutes until the next one.

I arrive at work, turn on the computer, put my lunch in the fridge and then my working day actually begins.

That probably all seems like a bit over the top for a commute, doesn't it? However, *this was how my mind worked* (without mindfulness). Filled with planning, filled with judgements, filled with lingering regrets, filled with problem-solving – even when the problems were as simple as getting to a window seat on the train. And, by the way, that was also the condensed version. Writing about all of my frustrations about the commute could have easily lasted longer than a chapter!

The main problem with that kind of thinking was it created an abundance of stress and didn't actually help me perform better at my work. I'm a notorious list maker, I'm well-organised and I strive to meet deadlines. I actually like a bit of a challenge! Thinking and worrying didn't help me do well at work, but it did help to create a few negatives. One: my working day felt like it lasted longer than it actually did. Two: I felt stressed and overwhelmed before I even arrived. Three: my worries were nearly always worse in my head than in reality so I wasted energy without needing to.

My experiences of commuting weren't of the actual commute itself. My experiences were of my thoughts about commuting. It's taken years to train my mind to create a more mindful attitude, and I hope that by sharing these stories, you can see just what a difference it can make.

Attitude two

The alarm goes off; I hop out of bed. I wash my face with warm water and appreciate the feeling of the soft face washer on my skin. I apply my makeup with brushes and pay attention to the texture of them.

In the car, I notice the colours of the sky as the sun starts to rise. If I need to stop at a red light, I take some deep breaths, feeling the air moving all the way into my body, down to my stomach and out again.

I might feel a twinge of worry when I have to stop at the second red light, but I remind myself that I'll still be able to catch the train (even though I might not have time to walk to my favourite carriage).

At the station, I feel my feet hitting the pavement as I walk down the two flights of stairs and along the platform.

When the train arrives, I get on and notice some seats (both at the window). I take a moment to feel glad that I can sit down.

Once I'm in my seat, I know I have half an hour to prepare myself for the working day. I check my social media and answer any pressing comments I've received during the night. I put in my headphones and listen to some of my favourite songs. I close my eyes so I can really pay attention to the words, the music and the feelings that the songs evoke. Sometimes, I look out the window and do my favourite mindful commuting challenge (to notice something I'd never noticed before). I often see people walking their dogs and feel cheered by the dog's obvious excitement to be out and about. I look at the clouds in the sky and notice the different shapes.

I haven't thought about the working day for more than a few seconds during that whole train ride.

I take the rest of the commute one step at a time. Get on the next train, exit the train, cross over the railway and start walking.

During the walk, I navigate my way around other people, while also noticing different aspects of the environment: little colourful flowers, cracks in the pavement, the ripening sky, wooden textures of the fences, freshly mown grass, the sounds of my feet hitting the ground, the feeling of the fresh air on my skin.

By the time I arrive at work, I actually feel quite content. I turn on my computer, put my lunch in the fridge and start my day by looking at the items on my to-do list and choosing a few priorities.

The truth is, experiencing a mindful commute is incredibly simple. But that doesn't mean it's easy! However, there are some really simple ways to practise mindfulness during the commute to (and from) work and I'm going to share these with you.

Even though I now work from home most of the time, I still use these practices whenever I do commute somewhere, or even when I'm just out and about. They're a great way to be more mindful and to find pockets of calm and meaning in everyday life.

Tips for mindful commuting

The 'Notice something new' challenge
Each time you commute to work, set yourself the challenge to notice something new. It could be a house you've never looked at before, a street name, the shape of leaves on a tree, a shop or an animal. Allow yourself to create the habit of paying attention to the world around you and exploring it with your eyes.

If you feel like there aren't enough new things to notice, or you'd like a change, then see if you can commute to work a different way! It may take a little longer, but it might also provide a richer experience.

Send out love

This is a practice I really enjoy doing when I've had a rough day, or when I'm feeling a bit flat. When I used to commute to and from work, I would literally see hundreds of people every trip and it was a great opportunity to tap into compassion and send good thoughts out into the world.

Simply rest your eyes on a person and think something along the lines of 'I'm sending you love' or 'I'm sending you compassion.' It only takes a second or two, but when there are more people, it becomes a challenge to keep up with everyone. And if someone notices you looking at them, perhaps just give them a smile – what a simple, beautiful gift at the end of a long day!

After a few minutes of this practice, I usually feel much lighter because I've enjoyed channelling my thoughts in a kind and positive way.

Connect with other people

Sometimes, connecting with other people can be as simple as making eye contact and sharing a smile. I used to miss out on this type of connection because I tended to look at the ground and avoided making eye contact with people. I'm not too sure why: perhaps a side effect of growing up in the country where there weren't so many people, or maybe it had something to do with being introverted. It could have been a habit I learned when I first moved to Melbourne and felt overwhelmed and nervous about the crowds!

During my psychology studies, I learned about a man who died by suicide from the Golden Gate Bridge in San Francisco, and how, in a note he left, he'd written that if one person smiled at him while he was en route, he wouldn't jump. That story reminded me that human connection doesn't only have to be reserved for the people we know. A small moment of connection between two strangers could truly mean something. I didn't want to keep missing those opportunities.

I now make it a challenge for myself to allow those mini-connections to unfold and to appreciate them when they happen.

Name colours

This is a really simple, yet effective, mindfulness practice. As the train sped along, I used to look around and name all the different colours I could see (even if the colours repeated a few times!).

You can also name the object that each colour belongs to. For example, blue and yellow seat covers, grey concrete, light-green leaves, a red roof, pale blue sky, a brown fence, green grass, pink flowers, a dark-grey building, an orange car ...

Continue with this practice for as long as you like and notice how it keeps you focused on the present moment, while also helping you simply see new information.

Mindful listening

If you enjoy listening to podcasts or music during the commute, spend some time really tuning in. You could close your eyes (as long as it's safe to do so and you're not likely to drift off and miss your stop!) and pay attention to the different instruments, pick out the beat, understand the lyrics and feel any emotions the song you're listening to evokes. If it's a cheerful song, it might make you feel uplifted. If it's a sad song, maybe it stirs feelings of loneliness or sorrow. Don't worry about your emotional response; it is simply your experience in the moment and it will pass.

The intention of this practice is to really listen on a deeper level and perhaps even explore if there are different elements within the song you've never noticed before.

Put your phone away

Have you ever found yourself mindlessly scrolling on your phone, not really looking at anything or paying attention, and then you seem to suddenly arrive at your destination without knowing where the last thirty minutes have gone? And maybe you do the same thing on the trip home, and again before you go to sleep. As confronting as it may be to realise, you might've spent around one and a half hours of your day scrolling mindlessly.

The accessibility and addictive nature of social media can literally drain away hours of your life which could have been spent in more productive, meaningful or purposeful ways!

The trick with using social media is to remain conscious about it: to use it in a way that is worthwhile, and to turn it off when mindlessness kicks in. I love connecting with people via social media, so I often use part of my commute to answer comments and create posts. Once I've finished using my phone, I like to close the cover and not open it back up again unless there's a reason. It can be tempting to just keep picking it up when we have a few spare moments (and this can quickly become a habit!), but why not direct your attention elsewhere – such as on a mindfulness practice?

Practise gratitude

The commute is a fantastic time to practise reframing your thoughts. You probably don't need to focus on much more than getting from Point A to Point B, and in the meantime you can think however you like!

While our minds tend to like searching for (and finding) negative aspects and focusing on those, we can quite literally change the way we think by using new thought patterns. In a 2016 study, participants who wrote letters focused on gratitude showed greater neural activity in the areas of the brain involved with gratitude.[1] This might not be surprising, but here comes the kicker: this activity was showing up *three whole months later*. So not only did their gratitude practice probably have positive short-term effects, such as a boost in happiness and a calmer attitude, there were also lasting benefits and actual changes in how their brain functioned over time.

As you begin your commute, try setting the intention to acknowledge and appreciate all the good things in your life, even things you might normally take for granted. Being able to use safe public transport. The weather. Hearing your favourite song on the radio if you're driving to work. Having some time to yourself. Arriving a little bit early. Anything you can feel a spark of gratitude for!

Journal

One of the most common questions I receive about journaling is how to make time for it. I know that setting aside five or ten minutes in the morning or evening can be difficult for people during busy times, which is why it's important to look for different opportunities to write. Journals are quite portable and the only other thing you'll need is a pen, which makes journaling quite an easy activity to do during the commute. Alternatively, you can write some notes on your phone or computer – there are even many different journaling apps you could try.

I've learned not to perceive the commute as a waste of time, but as an opportunity to do some of the sedentary things I don't always have a chance to do at home. I try to find conducive ways of spending my time during the commute, so that I can fit in more of the things I want to do in my life (like journaling and meditation).

CHAPTER 14

Enhancing productivity and mental clarity

Even though this chapter is about productivity and mental clarity, there's a question I'd like to ask you before we start exploring how to work more effectively.

Do you believe that your job is meaningful, rewarding or fulfilling *enough* to keep doing?

There are plenty of ups and downs with work, which is completely normal. Even if you have the most perfect job for you, which aligns with your ambitions and allows you to find meaning and purpose, it can still throw challenges at you. Challenges aren't necessarily bad; they can help you grow, learn new things, gain valuable skills and feel a sense of accomplishment. Your job might not feel meaningful, rewarding or fulfilling all the time. But is it enough of those things?

If your answer is no, then it may be time to start thinking about a job or career change (even if it won't happen straightaway).

There can be pressure to discover and chase after our dream careers, work incredibly hard to reach a certain point and then stick it out, no matter what. But we need to recognise when our jobs are no longer meaningful, rewarding or fulfilling enough and find the courage to make a change, knowing that we can never be certain what will happen next. Even though it may seem like there isn't a choice, there are many different opportunities out there. The next part of the journey may be wonderful, or it may be very challenging. We only have one life, though, and most of us will spend about 100,000 hours of that life at work. It's our own responsibility to do our best to make it feel worthwhile.

However, there are also times when jobs are simply a means of making money and supporting a family or a particular lifestyle. When I was studying full-time at university, I didn't particularly mind where I worked, as long as it allowed me to pay my bills. I worked in hospitality and retail and as a nanny, and I was grateful to have flexible jobs that supported me through that time in my life.

If you're in a position where you know you'd like to make a change (eventually), but it seems too impractical at this point in time, why not just set some goals and do more research so you'll be ready when a better time rolls around? You could enrol in an online course to further your knowledge, start building a network of people working in similar fields, attend workshops or events, create some of the things you might need (such as a resume or a website), or even see if you could undertake work experience for the job you'd like to have. I found that by doing things which would prepare me for the career I wanted to have, I felt like I had more purpose while I was working my necessary in-between jobs and I was more ready when the time came to actually start my new career!

Uncertainty and mindfulness

Feeling stuck? Not everyone knows exactly what they want to do and there are plenty of people in my life who are at a crossroads between realising they don't enjoy their current job and not knowing what to do next. If this is you, first of all, I just want to remind you that it's okay. No one can ever be 100 per cent sure about what will happen next in life! Even when we think we know for sure, we can still be surprised. It might feel incredibly uncomfortable to sit with the uncertainty, but try to look at it like this: uncertainty means a new adventure and a change in your life, which could work out to be more amazing than you could even imagine. However, for that to be a real possibility, you need to allow the uncertainty to unfold and use it to help you discover more about what you would like to do. Explore different ideas. Talk to other people. Complete personality tests to better understand your strengths. Look at the things you already love doing and investigate whether you could work (or create a business) in that area. I once read that nothing worth doing is ever easy and I do believe that chasing after a dream, committing to a change, learning and understanding new things and working towards something better takes courage and a whole lot of determination. There will be days when you'll feel like it isn't working. There will be days when you might reach a goal and feel on top of the world.

Going through a similar journey myself, I found that mindfulness truly supported me every step of the way. Creating a new career may seem like a rollercoaster ride, but it isn't. On a rollercoaster, you can just sit and let the ride take you wherever it wants, but this kind of journey takes so much more effort and intention than that! It's more like climbing over mountainous terrain; you know where you want to go, but there are many mountains to conquer and you'll likely stumble, fall, pick yourself up, keep moving, get stuck, go back and try another route – and little by little you'll continue moving forward. Along the way, you'll also see and experience some amazing things: feeling proud of how far you've come, realising you can achieve much more than you thought you could and finding new and unexpected (but totally rewarding!) mountains to climb.

Whenever you're feeling stuck, nervous, unsure, frustrated or hopeless, remember to practise mindfulness. Actually feel your emotion in your body and notice which thoughts it might have triggered. Observe, but try not to react. Essentially, create space for yourself to feel and experience that emotion fully, even if it's challenging and difficult to do so. It may be necessary to show yourself compassion by engaging in self-care, or taking some time to process your feelings and thoughts through meditation or journaling. Below, you'll find some questions to help you cultivate mindful awareness of challenging feelings. These questions are designed to help you simply observe your emotions and give them room to be felt (which often helps them to pass more quickly).

Just a little reminder before we get started – try to remain open-minded and nonjudgemental as you answer these questions. For example, rather than answering the question 'How am I feeling right now?' with 'I'm feeling frustrated and it's such a horrible feeling,' simply try to notice 'I'm feeling frustrated at the moment.'

- How am I feeling right now?
- Where can I feel this emotion most in my body?
- Has this emotion evoked a physical response?
- Has this emotion evoked a mental response? (Take note of which thoughts are coming up.)
- What can I say to become more accepting of this emotion? (For example, 'It's okay that I'm feeling this way' or 'I can accept that this is my experience right now.')
- How can I be more compassionate towards this emotion? (For example, you could say 'I understand why I'm feeling this way' or you could visualise holding the emotion with kindness.)
- Is there anything I can learn from this emotion right now?

You may like to finish this method of enquiry by repeating one, or all, of the following affirmations.

- This feeling is temporary and I can create the space to fully experience it.
- I am able to feel my emotions with self-compassion.

- I accept that this is my experience right now.
- My emotions are simply my experiences; they are not who I am.
- It is normal to feel a range of emotions.
- I embrace this feeling with curiosity, warmth and open-mindedness.
- I can experience my emotions without having to act on them.
- This moment is only one of many in my life; I can be open to it.

Mental clarity and productivity

Now that we've explored some of the thoughts, feelings and possibilities when it comes to work, we can begin to delve into mental clarity and productivity. I found that when I started working on my podcast, this book and other important aspects of my business, mental clarity and productivity became much more meaningful. I had to motivate myself, stick to my own deadlines, conquer creative blocks, maintain consistent productivity, enhance my mental clarity and really make the space for myself to create the best work I could.

Whatever your own work may be, mental clarity and productivity will help you get more done to a higher standard. This may lead to external rewards, such as a pay rise or recognition, but there are many internal rewards you can also experience, such as knowing you did your best, feeling proud of your efforts, having a sense of purpose and acknowledging the new skills you may have gained.

Mindfulness vs multi-tasking

Let's imagine you regularly go to a little coffee shop where a barista called Bob makes delicious coffee. Each day, he goes to work early in the morning, switches on the coffee machine and makes his first coffee. He feels passionate about the type of coffee he uses and enjoys implementing

163

his skills to create coffee art. As the day unfolds, he makes many different types of coffees. Even though he is busy, Bob puts time and care into each cup of coffee. If you stop long enough to watch, you'll see Bob pour the coffee beans into the grinder, fill the porta-filter (the tool that holds the coffee for the coffee machine), use a tamper to compress the coffee in the porta-filter, lock the porta-filter into the coffee machine and begin the extraction process. The result is a gorgeous cup of rich, aromatic, flavoursome coffee.

While this is just a little snapshot of Bob's coffee-making process, you can see how he attends to each of those steps with a level of focus. He's not thinking about other things, or counting down the hours until the end of the day, or wishing he was somewhere else.

Making coffee is often a mindful practice for Bob; he's present in the moment, paying attention to what's happening and taking each new step as it comes.

Now, imagine Bob has been given the responsibility of making the coffee, collecting payments from customers and delivering coffee to the tables. Basically, he's being asked to multi-task. You see Bob at the coffee machine, pouring the coffee beans into the grinder while he looks out the window, worrying about the customers who have been waiting for their coffee for too long. He burns the milk while collecting payment from a customer. He doesn't take the time to create coffee art because he's just moving as fast as he can. Accidentally, he gives the wrong amount of change to a customer. He goes back to making the coffees, completely lost on where he was up to. He's constantly trying to think a few steps ahead, predicting where the next problem may arise.

Multi-tasking in this way has drained the mindfulness away from Bob's coffee making (and more than likely increased his experience of stress). When people are interrupted during a work task, they often feel higher levels of stress as a result of frustration, mental workload and a sense of being under pressure. Interruptions at work also lengthen how long tasks take to complete because the worker has to reorient themselves back to the original task; ironically, this time is often compensated for by working faster – causing more stress!

Not only does multi-tasking have the potential to limit your experiences of mindfulness, it can also increase your levels of stress.[1] On the other hand, learning to focus specifically on one task more regularly can help enhance mental clarity and productivity by creating opportunities to concentrate and do things well the first time. It's important to try to reduce multi-tasking by delegating, asking for support, only taking on the amount of work you can handle and finding ways to minimise distractions, while incorporating a mindful attitude into the things you do.

Mindfulness and attention

Research has shown that meditation increases our ability to be efficient at work.[2] It slowly changes how our brains work by improving how long we can focus on a task and increasing our ability to avoid meaningless distractions.

For example, in a study in 1999 by Elizabeth Valentine and Philip Sweet, participants were asked to complete a test measuring their sustained attention skills (called Wilkins' counting test, which requires the participant to listen to sixty series of two to eleven bleeps and simply count the number of bleeps).[3] Some of the participants were long-term meditators (with more than twenty-four months of meditation experience), some were short-term meditators (with less than twenty-four months of meditation experience) and some had never meditated before. Both groups of meditators displayed a superior performance on the attention test than the group of people who had never meditated before. Also, the long-term meditators performed better than the short-term meditators. Another interesting result from the study was that mindfulness meditators (who practised mindfulness meditation as opposed to other types of meditation) performed better on the attention test when unexpected stimulus occurred. So while short-term meditation can be helpful in improving attention, the researchers found that long-term mindfulness meditation may have the greatest effects for maintaining attention.

By practising different forms of meditation regularly – such as mindfulness, breathing practices, visualisations, moving meditations and listening to meditation music – we can strengthen our ability to maintain attention, thereby improving productivity and mental clarity at work.

Finding mindful purpose

It can be easy to go to work each day and simply do what needs to be done, and repeat that process day in day out. However, it can bring a wonderful sense of purpose to your work if you regularly connect with your reasons for working and the meaning behind the things you do.

If I ask you 'Why do you do the work you do?', what would be your response?

- To earn money so you can support your family?
- To help make a difference?
- To support your travel adventures?
- To work towards a significant change?
- To create or build more interesting, fun and meaningful things for the world?

Once you know your purpose for being at work (you may also have a few different purposes!), see if you can connect with it each day. You could have a note about your purpose on a notepad to remind you, or set a password that helps you remember it. You could journal about how you worked towards your purpose at the end of each day. If you feel a little lost, take some time to think about what you could do to become more aligned with your purpose.

For example, when my podcast started to gain popularity, there was a rapid increase in the number of downloads it received. I began to focus on reaching the next download milestone: twenty thousand downloads, then fifty thousand, then one hundred thousand, then half a million and a million. I forgot that every single download was a real person listening to me as I shared my thoughts, experiences and ideas about mindfulness. I forgot that I wanted to guide and support people towards more mindful living. I forgot that I started the podcast without a care about downloads, just hoping I could reach and (maybe even help) one person. Ultimately, I forgot about my purpose.

One day, I reached a new milestone with my downloads and it didn't feel exciting any more – it simply felt like a number. And I started to doubt what I was doing and whether I should continue.

After a long walk with my partner and a lot of talking, I finally realised why podcasting had started to feel empty, despite the outward success. I just didn't feel connected to my purpose any more.

I read back over old emails and messages I'd received from some of the people I'd helped on their mindfulness journeys and I began to recognise each download for what it was; not just a number, but an actual person. Almost immediately, I felt the shift from lacking purpose and meaning to feeling motivated and excited about what I was doing.

Sometimes, all it takes is a change in perspective to help us rediscover our purpose and keep working towards it!

CHAPTER 15

The assertive employee

When I was a little girl, maybe four or five years old, someone I knew thought it would be funny to pick me up and hold me over a small pond, lowering me closer and closer until my dress got wet. While he meant it as a joke, I felt totally overwhelmed by my lack of power and I felt ashamed and embarrassed. I ran and hid under a desk, wishing I could disappear.

I watched people searching for me and heard them calling my name, but I didn't move. I just wanted to be on my own, where I felt safe.

The 'flight' response was almost always my way of coping with challenges in life. Whenever a problem or conflict arose, I escaped. If I was feeling vulnerable emotions, like anger or guilt, I squashed them down rather than express them. If I started to feel like I was failing at something, I gave up. I avoided people if we weren't on good terms, only ever feeling able to fully express myself through writing – sometimes I wrote letters, sometimes I just made notes in my journals.

Slowly but surely, I realised that I didn't need to keep running away from people, as long as they never felt angry with me. So I became the ultimate people-pleaser. When I made mistakes, I lied to make myself look good. I believed that if I always tried to do the right thing – or made it seem like I was doing the right thing even when I wasn't – then I could keep my 'flight' response under control.

If I worked really hard on my assignments at school, my teachers would be pleased. If I kissed my boyfriend whenever he wanted, he'd think I was great. If I was quiet and sensible, my parents would be proud of me. If I let my friends make all the decisions about how we spent our time, they'd keep being my friends.

And then there was work.

If I arrived early to get more things done, my colleagues would be appreciative. If I didn't take time off, my boss would be happy with me. If I took on extra shifts (even when I didn't want to), I'd receive praise for being 'hardworking'.

Or at least, that's what I told myself. The truth, however, was that being a people-pleaser, a pushover and a 'yes-woman' actually created three main problems for me as an employee.

One, I felt bitter and resentful when I agreed to things I didn't want to agree to and I enjoyed my work a lot less. Two, I was constantly worried about making a mistake, like arriving late or saying the wrong thing. And three, I regularly felt burned out. Basically, I didn't respect my own wants and needs in the workplace and I became an often unhappy, stressed and exhausted employee.

Fortunately, many of the places I worked at were great and they looked out for me and tried to meet my needs, even when I didn't vocalise them. But there came a time when I realised I had to grow up.

My great-aunt died by suicide and I went to work the next day after an awful night's sleep and a lot of tears. I agonised for hours about asking my boss if I could take a day off during the week to attend the funeral – and when I finally got the courage, she gently chastised me for going into work that day. She told me I could go home. When I did return to work, I found flowers on my desk. She also said I could take a day off for the funeral – that, actually, I should take as many days as I needed to spend some time with my family.

I remember feeling grateful for her kindness and understanding, but also disappointed with myself. I'd considered missing the funeral just because I was too worried about asking for an unexpected day off. And I'd gone to work during a time when I knew I needed to grieve, and when I could have been spending time with my family as they grieved.

I decided that I had to start taking my own wellbeing at work seriously and the best way for me to do that was to speak up. If I needed a day off unexpectedly, I had to ask for it. If I knew there was a better way to do things, I had to explain how. If too much was being asked of me, then I had to say so.

But how could I do that without getting fired and without starting a conflict? How could I ensure that my needs were being met, while also being a good employee?

Funnily enough, I already knew the answer!

I'd heard about assertiveness quite a few times during my psychology studies and helpline training, and read about it in a number of self-help books. I knew that if I could become a more assertive employee, it would benefit everyone around me (and myself, too!).

If you're at all like me and the idea of being assertive is enough to get your heart racing, there's no need to be afraid. Assertiveness is an incredibly empowering skill and it allows us to clearly convey our needs, while boosting resilience and decreasing stress in the long-term.

You might like to re-visit Chapter 4 and pillar three (about honesty and assertiveness) for a refresher about what assertiveness is and why it's so important. Everything you learned about how to be assertive can also be applied to the workplace and your life as an employee (or employer). Here a few examples.

Action tips for being assertive at work

Take breaks when you're supposed to
Are you not taking your allocated breaks at work? Maybe it's busy whenever you want to take your break, or your to-do list is long, or you put pressure on yourself to keep working. For whatever reason, it isn't fair. You are entitled to your breaks and it's your responsibility to make sure you take them.

Keep in mind that breaks will often help you feel refreshed so that you can return to your work in a better mood. Not only will your work potentially be of a higher standard, but you might feel happier or calmer than before the break.

Only answer emails when you're at work
One of my rules when I worked in an office job was that I didn't answer work emails at home. I had my own business at the time too, and this forced me to get strict with how I spent my time – if I was at home, then my priorities were my business and my family and my self-care activities. I noticed that when I checked work emails at home, I felt tempted to deal with them (even when they weren't urgent). So I set myself the rule that I simply wouldn't check those emails at home.

It's quite simple to set up out-of-office email replies that provide an alternative contact person, so that anything urgent can still be dealt with whenever you aren't there. I highly recommend that you let your boss or colleagues know your intentions and set up that email.

Say no to extra shifts when you don't want them
If someone asks you to take on an extra shift and you are genuinely willing and able to take on that shift, then feel free to do it. But if you aren't willing or able, then it's your right to say no. It's okay to simply say 'No, thank you, I won't be able to do that extra shift.' You don't need to provide them with excuses or reasons!

If you ever feel bullied or blackmailed into working extra shifts, then it might be a good idea to have a conversation about it with the appropriate person. You might want to acknowledge the situation with the person who keeps requesting you to take on extra shifts, or if you're really concerned, you may need to talk about it with someone with more authority.

Take annual leave or sick leave
Annual leave and sick leave are there for you for very good reasons: it's not in the best interest of the company to have sick people at work (where they could potentially spread germs with others) or to have employees who feel burned out simply because they haven't taken proper time off. Nor is it in your best interest to go to work when you're unwell because it could delay your recovery, not to mention the fact that you probably won't be working to the best of your ability.

Try to give your employer as much notice as you can, but if an emergency pops up, remember that life happens and it's okay to take time off then, too. Keep in mind that it's in everyone's best interest for you to be feeling capable, focused and well at work.

Delegate tasks

Constantly feeling swamped and overwhelmed by the amount of work you have to do? Some people take on more than they can handle at work and end up making sacrifices in other important areas of their life just to get everything done. If this is you, then it might be a good idea to look at how you can delegate some tasks.

Could you hand over some projects to someone who might have time to help you? Could you talk to your employer about hiring an assistant? Could you simply say 'no' to taking on as much work as you do, so it can be delegated to someone else in the first place?

Ask for a raise

Do you honestly feel that you're being paid what you deserve to be paid for your work? If not, then it's time to have an open conversation with your employer about the possibility of a raise. Let them know how you've grown in the role and how you add value to the position. Be honest about the work you put in and ask if there's potential for you to receive a raise.

If they say yes, that's great! If they say no, at least you know where you stand and you can make an informed decision about what to do next.

Request support when you need it

You may require different levels of support at various times in your career. Many companies are able to provide certain types of support, such as discounted counselling services, help with childcare costs, carer's leave, and more. Whatever you might need support with, check out the company policies and don't be afraid to ask for further information.

Go home on time

I understand that sometimes, it can be necessary to stay late at work. However, if you regularly find yourself putting in extra unpaid hours and you're often late to leave, then it's time to look at your options. Could you delegate some tasks, ask to be paid for the extra time, or simply leave when you're supposed to (even if you haven't quite finished your to-do list)?

You might like to have an honest conversation with your boss – perhaps they aren't even aware of the extra time you're putting in! Let them know which action you would prefer to take, or ask if they have any suggestions.

Working late regularly is often an unsustainable way of getting things done; you might slowly become exhausted, overworked, frustrated or resentful. Not to mention what you might be missing out on at home: a chance to rest and recover; quality time with loved ones; or activities that benefit your wellbeing, such as exercise and sleep.

Deal with inappropriate behaviour

There are various types of inappropriate behaviours that can occur at work, including unwanted physical contact, spreading rumours, discrimination, unreasonable work-related demands, offensive comments, unjustified criticism, deliberate exclusion of people in the workplace and aggressive (or abusive) behaviour. According to Safework Australia, 9.4 per cent of Australian workers indicated that in the last six months, they had experienced bullying in the workplace (2014–15).

Everyone should have the right to feel valued, safe and comfortable at work, so if you don't, then it's time to do something about it.

Find the right people to talk to and be honest about your experiences. Allow those people who can help you to hear you – no one can help if they don't know what you've been facing. And know that if you feel unsafe at any time, you need to do what's best for your wellbeing and leave.

Leave your job
Being assertive about leaving a job can be difficult to do. I never found it easy, often feeling an immense amount of guilt and trying to put it off for as long as possible. However, it's important to remember that leaving a job is your choice. Only you can decide when it's time to go and even though it can be hard and you might feel uncertain, you owe it to yourself to do what feels right (or necessary).

It's also important to say no if, at the point of leaving, your employer asks you for anything you don't feel comfortable with. They may ask you to remain with the company as a casual employee, or request that you stay longer than your required notice period, or want you to be an ongoing contact for the new employee to call if they need guidance. You may like to think about these questions and be prepared with your assertive answers.

CHAPTER 16

Mindfulness techniques for stress

When I was invited to speak at my first event, I said yes despite a deluge of fear and self-doubt. The only times I'd spoken in public were during high school and those were not memories I felt fond of. Actually, thinking about them was enough to start my stomach churning with dread.

As the event drew closer, my nerves grew and grew. However, I consciously practised mindfulness whenever I noticed myself overthinking or planning the worst. I'd be lying in bed at night starting to imagine my mind going blank on stage, and then I'd refocus on the present moment by practising a breathing technique. It may not seem like much, but using breathing techniques had a soothing and calming effect on me and helped me disconnect from my catastrophising thoughts for long enough to realise that they weren't helping me.

When the event rolled around, I'd practised my speech enough to know I could get through it and I'd created cue cards in the chance I'd get lost for words. I felt prepared, but scared. However, I was also proud of the way I'd taken care of my mental health in the lead-up to the event.

With twenty minutes to go before I was due on stage, the full force of my nerves struck and I could feel myself starting to panic. My heart was pounding. I felt like I could hardly breathe. My hands were shaking. I couldn't focus. My stomach felt like it was tying itself up in knots. I was sweating, but every now and then I felt a strange chill run up my spine, making me shiver. I was ready to run.

I started walking slowly along the corridor, forcing myself to take big, deep breaths while I noticed three things I could see, three things I could hear and three things I could feel. When I finished one round of tuning into some of my senses, I started again, noticing three new things I could see, hear and feel.

By the time I walked on stage, I actually felt okay. Not great! But okay. As soon as I started my speech, I tried to use my cue cards and focused on making eye contact with people, pausing to breathe and using my hands to help me tell my story. There was a little moment about halfway through when I remember thinking 'Wow, I think I might actually be enjoying this.'

I'm sure it wasn't a perfect presentation, but I'd done it. I'd survived my first voluntary public speaking event.

Since then, I've experimented with managing stress at work in various ways. I've used breathing techniques in the bathroom after challenging phone calls. When I have started worrying on a Sunday afternoon about going back to work the next morning, I've refocused on the present moment. I've gone for mindful walks on my breaks and completed a few simple stretches to help relieve tension headaches. I've written to-do lists that triggered a sense of being overwhelmed, but rather than multi-tasking (like I used to!) I've learned to concentrate on one thing at a time.

The more I've used mindfulness techniques to help me manage stress, the more I've been able to enjoy my work, switch off at home, tap into a sense of calm (even during hectic times) and take better care of myself, both physically and mentally. In this chapter, I'm going to share all my favourite mindfulness strategies for stress at work, and also stress about work.

Stress at work

It's not uncommon to feel stress in the workplace. There are a number of individual factors that can contribute to feelings of stress: your stress-tolerance, the amount of sleep you've been getting, your responsibilities (both at home and at work), tight deadlines, pressure from your colleagues, difficult projects and long hours. Not being appreciated at work and feeling unheard can also contribute to work stress. I could go on and on about the rising panic created by an overflowing email inbox or a never-ending to-do list, but I think you get the gist!

The truth is, work can be stressful in a variety of different ways. Even if you love the work you do, it can still provide challenges that you may not always feel ready for. And while a little bit of stress can be a good thing because it may help motivate you, ongoing stress at work has the potential to cause bigger problems, like lack of sleep, a compromised immune system and the potential to cause an anxiety disorder to develop.

Simone's story

Before Simone learned how be more mindful, she'd worry herself sick if her boss scheduled a private meeting with her in their office the next day. She was sure she was going to get into trouble, or be told she'd done something wrong. But then she started practising mindfulness. Simone realised that jumping to the worst possible conclusion could completely ruin her day, when more often than not, there was actually nothing to be concerned about. Or if there was, there was nothing she could do about it by having a sleepless night – it would just make her less able to discuss the matter rationally with her boss the next day. Simone used a variety of mindfulness techniques, including breathing techniques and observing her thoughts (rather than reacting to them).

Mindfulness has shown her that there isn't much point wasting energy stressing about the things she doesn't yet know or can't control; instead, she focuses on the work at hand and deals with potential issues when they arrive. Alternatively, if she's really concerned about something, she asks the person involved if they can address the issue right away to help clear her mind. Using mindfulness has helped Simone manage stressful days and confrontation at work and it's helped her better understand how to approach challenging situations in order to avoid becoming upset unnecessarily.

Mindfulness practices for stress at work

Spend time around nature

Another simple way to manage stress at work is to increase your exposure to nature. Research has shown that the more an employee is exposed to nature, the lower their experiences with stress and depression are (and the more likely they are to feel job satisfaction).[1] The great news about becoming more exposed to nature is that it's fairly easy to implement on a regular basis. Try opening the blinds to allow sunlight into the workplace, buy some indoor plants, or go for walks outside whenever you have work breaks (or walk to and from work, if you can). Engage with nature in a mindful way by noticing the different colours, textures, shapes and details and, if you're outside, try to notice the aromas and sounds and the feeling of the solid ground beneath your feet.

If you have a spare ten minutes on your lunch break, try going for a mindful walk along a tree-lined street, through a park, or anywhere else that helps expose you to nature. Allow your mind to gently settle on the different aspects of nature around you and explore all the sensations that might arise for you. If you notice your mind wandering back to your work, gently return it to the present moment by noticing your breath and then expanding your awareness to the world around you again.

Take mindful breaks

Another way to manage stress at work is to take regular, mindful breaks. Because I spend most of my working time at a desk in front of a computer, I try to surround myself with objects and tools I can use during my mindful breaks, rather than picking up my phone and scrolling through social media! When I consciously take mindful breaks, I can check in with how I'm feeling, give my mind a rest and allow stress to be released.

A few things I keep at my desk include an aromatic mist spray, a coconut-scented hand cream, a meaningful quote in a frame, a variety of little plants, a journal and pen, a glass of water and a hand massager. About once per hour, I try to use at least one of these objects in a mindful way. I might squeeze some cream onto my hands and appreciate the coconut smell and the smooth texture. I'll read the quote and notice how it makes me feel. I'll sprinkle a little bit of water on my plants and observe the way they look. If I'm feeling a little lost or uninspired, I might write a few sentences in my journal about what I'm grateful for. These regular mindful breaks may seem small or insignificant, but they make a big difference to how I feel throughout the day.

Emily's story

Emily works for a non-profit organisation which grants heartfelt wishes for children living with life-threatening illnesses. Even though she feels that her work is incredibly rewarding, it can also be challenging and stressful at times, such as the lead-up to large fundraising events. Emily has started to incorporate mindfulness practices into her working day, especially when she feels like stress is being triggered. She uses breathing techniques, goes for mindful walks on her breaks, focuses on her senses and works on one task at a time (instead of regularly multi-tasking and feeling overwhelmed!). Most days, she might use just one or two of these practices, but she still notices the benefits, such as lower stress and greater productivity.

Emergency mindfulness practices

Even when we try to manage stress by taking mindful breaks and exposing ourselves to nature, there can still be moments of high stress and pressure that overwhelm us. You might disagree with a colleague, make a serious mistake, be inundated by urgent requests, receive an email that sets an unrealistic deadline, or hear negative feedback about your work from someone you respect. In any situation that triggers a strong stress response, there are a number of mindfulness practices which can be particularly helpful.

Mindful breathing

As you may have guessed, mindful breathing is always my first go-to activity when I'm feeling overwhelmed. I find it to be such a powerful way of calming myself down and reconnecting with my more rational mind (instead of overreacting and escalating my stress response with negative thoughts).

One of the great things about this mindful activity is that you can practise it anywhere, anytime – and it's likely that no one will even notice!

Simply become aware of your breath and pay attention to the journey of it as it travels through your nose, throat, chest and diaphragm (and back out again). If mindful breathing isn't enough, you can also try taking deeper breaths. Focus on drawing as much air into your lungs as feels comfortable, hold it for a moment and then release the breath, trying to make the exhale last longer than the inhale. To ensure that you exhale all the way, gently squeeze your stomach muscles towards the end of your breath because this will encourage deeper breathing.

Soothing touch

Place one hand over the part of your body where you feel the most stress. For me, this tends to be my chest or stomach. Notice the warmth of your hand and the gentle pressure of it against your body. If it feels soothing to you, feel free to gently rub the area in small circles, or imagine a warm light emanating from your hand into that stressed area of your body. If you choose to picture the warm light, you can also experiment with visualising the stress melting away from the area; you might picture it as a dark sticky substance like tar that will melt and dissolve, or a hot red liquid that evaporates and disappears.

Progressive muscle relaxation

The aim of this strategy is to systematically isolate and tense your muscles, and then release the tension while paying close attention to the sensation of relaxation.

For example, you might start with your feet by squeezing all the muscles in that area and then releasing them. You can continue up your entire body – your lower legs, upper legs, groin and buttocks, stomach, chest, upper back, upper arms, lower arms and hands. You can then do one final squeeze using your entire body and allow yourself to sink into the floor or seat, becoming heavy and relaxed.

Alternatively, you can choose particular muscles that you know tense up when you're stressed and focus on deliberately squeezing and relaxing them.

Be careful not to tense your muscles so much that you feel pain or discomfort; the aim is simply to experience a sense of relaxation.

Stress about work

Being *at* work isn't the only time we can feel stressed about it. As someone who used to check emails as soon as they landed in my inbox (even if it was 10 pm and I was already in bed) and who used to feel more and more worried as the weekend came to each inevitable end, I know what it's like to feel stressed *about* work. I could be watching a movie at home on the couch and be distracted by an upcoming project deadline. I could be taking a shower and ruminating over something I didn't get right. I could be eating breakfast at a café and feel the sudden urge to check emails.

Work stress doesn't just appear when we're physically in the workplace; it can be triggered at any time and can be really difficult to let go of.

Practising mindfulness has made a massive difference in reducing the amount of stress I feel about work when I'm not actually there. I'm able to quickly identify when my thoughts are running away and remind myself that since I'm not at work, it's not something I need to think about in that moment.

Learning to let go of stress about work is definitely an ongoing process; I found it incredibly difficult at first and the more I practised, the easier it became. There were a few things I did that helped me let go of stress about work: turning off email notifications on my phone and not checking my inbox until I was at work, keeping a to-do list for work so I could write down important things I need to remember, maintaining open communication with my colleagues to create realistic deadlines that didn't require me to work extra hours at home – and, of course, practising mindfulness.

Mindfulness practices for stress about work

Letting go of 'work-solving'

One of the things I used to do when I wasn't at work was predict and problem-solve in advance any possible issues that could occur at work in the future. I call this 'work-solving'.

In my spare time when I could have been enjoying self-care, or spending time with my loved ones, or really just living my life outside of work, I'd be work-solving. I'd lie in bed in the morning and at night and work-solve. I'd be relaxing in the bath and start work-solving. I'd be hanging out with my friends or family and start talking about work so I could work-solve with them!

I was a work-solve-aholic.

Learning to let go of my work so I could be more present in the other areas of my life has been a huge relief. It allows me to be present in the moment without the distraction of thinking about work on a regular basis.

The practice for this might sound easy in theory, but it can be particularly difficult to do. Anytime you notice yourself work-solving, firmly remind yourself that it's not the time and reconnect with the present moment. For example, if you're taking a shower and you realise that you're work-solving, guide your attention to the warmth of the water, the aromas of soap or hair products, the sound of the water splashing around you and the feeling of your feet on the floor. A simple thing I do to refocus when I'm in the shower is to create a cup with my hands, then imagine the water in my pretend cup is filled with my work-solving thoughts. Once the water starts to overflow, I release it and allow it all to wash away.

Participating in engaging activities

If you're finding it especially difficult to let go of stress about work, it can be really helpful to participate in an activity that grabs your attention. As we will explore more in Chapter 18, fun and creative activities can facilitate mindful awareness by grabbing our interest and encouraging an immersive state of flow. Think about the last time you engaged in an activity you really enjoyed – was it easy to focus on the present moment and let go of work stress? If yes, then this could be a great activity to engage in whenever you're feeling overwhelmed by worries about work. If not, then try to think of another activity you could use to focus your attention on the present moment. If you're feeling stuck for ideas, then sit tight because we'll be diving deep into the topic of fun and creativity in the next part of this book!

PART SIX

Hobbies, Fun and Creativity

CHAPTER 17

The pursuit of fun

In her book *Big Magic*, Elizabeth Gilbert noted that 'at the end of your days, you can thank creativity for having blessed you with a charmed, interesting and passionate existence'.[1]

It really is incredible how much human beings actually express creativity, not just in the more traditionally identified forms of creativity, such as painting and drawing, but in many different ways – from creative thinking to decorating our homes or colour-coordinating our outfits.

As someone who tended to believe I 'wasn't very creative', after reading Elizabeth Gilbert's book, I realised that my creativity was showing up every single day in unexpected ways. Meal planning, meditating, organising my home, journaling, taking photos, doing my hair and makeup, posting on social media …

It turns out that I am creative and I've come to realise that it's a part of my life that enhances my happiness and fulfilment (and presents an amazing opportunity to practise mindfulness – more on that later!). Gone are the days of looking at the beautiful artwork my sister creates and feeling a sense of sadness for the 'creative talent' I thought I was missing.

The interesting thing was, as soon as I started to believe in my own creativity, the more I looked for and took new chances to express it.

In Christmas 2017, I decided to DIY the majority of my Christmas gifts by making bath bombs, my own version of Baileys (a coffee and chocolate creamy alcoholic drink) and nearly fifty origami envelopes containing date cards for my partner. At the same time, I was experimenting with brewing my own kombucha and making coconut yoghurt, while doing various creative tasks for my work (including writing this book!). It felt so exciting and fulfilling to be surrounded by things I'd made and to use my spare time experimenting and working on new ideas.

Creativity is all about using your imagination, or different ways of thinking, to be more inventive. Take a moment to think about the various ways you've expressed your own creativity over the last week. Have you cooked meals? Put together an outfit? Solved a problem by thinking outside the box? Played music? Written an email?

You may be surprised by just how much creativity is woven into your everyday life!

The potential benefits of creativity are vast and varied, which is something I find to be truly exciting. A study by Bradley Fisher and Diana Specht in 1999 found that creative activities can help promote successful ageing by facilitating a sense of competence, purpose and growth.[2] Thirty-six people between the ages of sixty and ninety-three years took part in this study by participating in a senior art exhibition. They were then interviewed about the benefits of creativity and its relationship to successful ageing. The results demonstrated that artistic creativity not only contributed to the participants' feelings of competence, purpose and growth, creativity also helped them develop their problem-solving skills and motivation in managing everyday life. While this study wasn't particularly rigorous, I think it beautifully sums up what creativity can do for us; it allows us to develop, learn and grow throughout life and helps us feel purposeful and motivated.

A multitude of research has also shown benefits such as innovation, open-mindedness and flexibility – demonstrating that creativity doesn't just contribute to positive feelings and experiences, but is actually entwined with useful ways of thinking!

The big wall that can separate a person from expressing their creativity is often their beliefs about it, and I can absolutely attest to this!

'I can't do that, I'm not creative enough.'

'There's no point trying this new creative activity – I don't have the talent.'

'I'm too practical for creativity and I'd rather spend my time more efficiently.'

'Everyone else is going to be great at this and whatever I create will be awful.'

Sound familiar? If so, never fear. I've been there (and still find myself there from time to time!). The wonderful thing about thoughts like these is that they can change and morph into new beliefs that support us to not only try to be more creative, but to actually see the beauty of the experience, rather than the outcome.

For example, when I was a young girl, a relative of mine shared her opinion of my singing voice. It wasn't a particularly kind opinion and I took it completely to heart. I was so embarrassed about my lack of singing ability that even though I went on to play music and write songs throughout my childhood and teenage years, I tried to avoid singing in front of other people as much as possible.

Nearly twenty years after the remark about my voice, I met my partner who believes that everyone should sing. He often sings around the house, makes up his own lyrics and encourages other people to sing, too. Including me. 'I'm a terrible singer. Honestly, no one wants to hear me sing,' I told him. After much encouragement and a slow shift in my own beliefs, I began to sing more and more: while I was cooking, when we were driving with the radio on, in the shower ... I may not be lovely to listen to or have a future career as a singer, but that doesn't mean I can't (or shouldn't) do it. It's a creative way for me to have fun and laugh. And I feel a sense of liberation from having to be great at it; instead, I do it just because it makes me happy.

Next time you find yourself thinking 'I can't', try to add a little caveat: 'I can't YET.' And then just give it a go and see what you can learn and how you can grow.

Letting go

Engaging in hobbies and trying new creative activities is something that can bring so much joy and fulfilment, but for that to happen, we often need to learn to let go of a few things:

- perfectionism and the need to be successful straightaway
- comparing ourselves to others
- needing a reason or point for engaging in a hobby (other than having fun!)
- the outcome by focusing on the journey instead.

By using mindfulness techniques to help us let go, we can empower ourselves and genuinely allow those needs of perfectionism and pressure and comparison to gently pass. The practice of mindfulness calls for nonjudgement, which is such an important element of embracing the 'beginner' stage. Also, without judgement, we can see so much more. We can see when we need to be kinder towards ourselves and when we might need a break. We can see new ways of learning, rather than just feeling frustrated and stuck. We can see when we're indulging negative thoughts and then, hopefully, choose to invite more positive thoughts into our minds.

Mindfulness for letting go

Let's imagine you've decided to try a new hobby, such as snowboarding. Maybe you went on a school camp when you were ten years old and tried snowboarding as part of the organised activities. You really enjoyed it, but never had a chance to do it again. Well now, you have that chance!

You do some research and discover a snowfield not too far away from you and you decide to visit. When the day rolls around, you start to wonder if you should be wasting your time when there are so many other more important things to do.

Let me just pause the story here for a moment. 'Wasting time' is something I often hear about in relation to creative activities or hobbies (and I used to feel a similar way myself). However, having fun is not time wasted. Learning something new is not time wasted. Going out of your comfort zone and learning new skills is definitely not time wasted!

Giving yourself permission to engage in a hobby can positively impact your life in various ways, such as meeting new people (potentially improving your social wellbeing) and enhancing happiness and creativity. Research has also shown that engaging in hobbies has been linked to protective health factors, such as lower blood pressure (particularly when the hobby incorporates exercise) and less stress.[3] It's important to remember that spending time on hobbies and fun activities may not always result in obvious 'progress', but there are various other ways it could be benefiting you and your wellbeing.

So, back to the snowboarding story. You've noticed yourself worrying that you'll be wasting your time on the snowboarding adventure, but you're not sure what to do next. Here are two simple mindfulness practices you can use at any time during your adventures to help you let go of thoughts about wasting your time (or any other judgements). These mindfulness practices can also help you create a richer, more mindful experience as your adventures unfold.

1: *Learn the lessons*

We are always learning lessons. If you become dehydrated and get a headache, you might learn to drink more water. If you go to bed at 1 am and struggle to get out of bed for work, you'll learn to go to bed earlier. If you take a wrong turn on your drive to work and it gets you there faster, you'll learn a better route. Learning a lesson is a great thing because it means you're growing in some way.

However, many people become frustrated during the process of learning a new hobby. They might feel overwhelmed by thoughts of being 'stupid' or 'bad', or wonder why they aren't mastering something fast enough, or wish they could skip the learning to achieve the mastery.

This mindfulness practice is all about embracing the learnings.

Any time you observe yourself learning or growing in any way (even if the lesson is tough!), try to acknowledge it.

For example, imagine you're at the snowfield and trying to fit your feet into the snowboarding boots. It's a tight fit and you worry they'll be too uncomfortable, so you take the boots back. Fortunately, the assistant lets you know that tight boots are important when snowboarding to stop your feet from sliding around inside. You acknowledge to yourself, 'There's a lesson; snowboarding boots should be firm to stop my feet from sliding around.'

Once you start moving, you fall over almost straightaway. Then again. And again. You take a moment to watch other snowboarders and notice that they bend at the knees. You acknowledge, 'Lesson learned; bend at the knees.'

Even though you feel more balanced, you realise that snowboarding is much harder than it looks! You decide to book in with an instructor who can help you learn the basics. 'This is a great lesson,' you think. 'It's a good idea to find support when I'm trying challenging, new things.'

By the end of the day, you've learned many more lessons and you've managed to stay upright on the snowboard for more than a few metres at a time – not an easy task for a first (or second) attempt at snowboarding!

By acknowledging our lessons, we can appreciate our own journeys and growth, while learning to refrain from judgement and comparison. It can be a deeply rewarding mindfulness practice to use whenever you're engaging in a hobby, because, chances are, you'll continue learning more and more – but it's likely the lessons will become gradually more challenging as you gain new skills!

Furthermore, 'learning the lessons' helps us take things one step at a time by simply learning one lesson at a time. This helps reduce any pressure we might feel to become great at something straightaway and also enhances the positive side of making mistakes. The more we can turn a mistake into an opportunity to learn, the more we will be likely to enjoy and appreciate the experience.

2: Mind your movements

Hobbies tend to involve movements of some kind. Knitting, drawing and playing piano tend to require hand movements. Ice skating, dancing, horseriding and rock climbing involve our whole bodies. Stargazing and birdwatching encourage us to look around, moving our heads and eyes.

As you do the different movements of your chosen hobby, notice how it actually feels. It might help to label the movements as you do them, or you might like to simply observe the different sensations that arise in your body.

For example, when you start to get the hang of snowboarding, you may find a nice flow of shifting the weight between your legs to help turn the board as you go down the mountain. As you notice the movements, you could describe them to yourself: 'I'm putting my weight back into my heels to gain control, I'm taking the weight off my heels slightly, I'm swinging my left leg behind me until I've turned enough …' Alternatively, you can just immerse yourself in the experience of those movements.

I find that when the hobby I'm doing is fairly simple (like walking), I like to mind my movements by *labelling* them – this prevents me from being distracted. I also do it when I'm learning something new and challenging (such as abseiling), when I have to really concentrate.

When I'm doing an activity that I'm fairly confident about, such as cooking, yoga and photography, I prefer to mind my movements by simply *feeling* them.

Feel free to experiment and see which technique (labelling or feeling) resonates most with you and keep in mind that your preference may also change depending on the activity.

Having fun

Sometimes I think I take life a bit too seriously. I get swept up in the importance of doing things right, of making good decisions and ensuring that I'm focused on my goals. I forget about having fun.

A while ago, I was watching a documentary featuring a Brazilian chef named Alex Atala, who recalled a dream he'd had about the meaning of life.[4] In the dream, he was being guided by someone bigger than he was, who said the meaning of life was about circles. He showed Alex a flower and then described the life cycle of a plant. Each plant has a circle, the man said: a seed grows and becomes a plant, which creates a flower that becomes a fruit, then the fruit drops and leaves behind another seed. And Alex said he understood, but he wanted to know why the man showed him the flower rather than the seed or the fruit. And the man replied, 'The flower is the moment that we live, the most beautiful moment of the circle. The most beautiful moment.'

I believe that having fun is our opportunity to make the most of our own beautiful moments: to say yes to things that bring us joy, to smile and laugh, to be grateful for the sparks of connection with others, to discover real purpose and to embrace our individuality and what makes us unique.

It's not always easy to let go of the seriousness or to put aside the to-do list (especially when life gets busy!). Mindfulness practices can be so helpful in allowing us to become more present and to let go of judgemental thoughts that can interfere with our experiences of having fun. Choose a fun activity you can engage in (even if it's only for a few minutes) and try to approach it mindfully by paying attention to your experience and bringing your mind back to the present moment.

CHAPTER 18

Why is creativity important?

It would be difficult to count all the hundreds of ways that creativity has enriched my life, but there is one particular instance that immediately comes to mind.

I must have been seven or eight years old when I first decided to write my own book. I had the idea to create a story about a girl who travelled all around the world, meeting new people and having wonderful adventures. I created folders to collect information about all the different countries she would visit and I wrote perhaps a chapter or two before I lost interest in the face of a new (and therefore, better!) idea.

I kept writing, though: chapters of stories, journals, poems. When I was eleven, I entered a story into a competition as part of a school project and it was selected as a finalist, which allowed me to attend a day event about writing. I was so proud of my story and it fulfilled a huge part of a dream which, at that stage, had really just begun.

Over the years, I continued writing. Not because I felt like I had to or because other people said I should. I wrote because it allowed me to express my ideas and thoughts, to feel excited about the possibility of a new story, to achieve something that felt truly meaningful to me.

I have notebooks filled with ideas for stories, snippets of chapters, poems, song lyrics and journaling ventures. I continue to write because it adds real value to my life, even if there's no obvious external reward.

In 2014, I started my first blog and the new opportunities to write astounded and completely excited me. I entered the blogging world with enthusiasm, submitting articles that were published in *The Huffington Post* and *The New York Times*. On my own blog, I shared my experiences with stress and mindfulness, as well as techniques and ideas I'd learned during my psychology studies.

In 2017, I began writing this book. As one of the first goals I'd written down at the start of my blogging journey three years before, this book is much more than just a creative process for me. However, creativity is where it all started from and it's also what has guided me through all my years of writing.

I felt curious about what I could build with words: journals, blog posts, interviews, stories, poems. And as I explored this curiosity, I noticed other benefits of being creative in this way:

- gaining knowledge in the field of psychology (which I used to improve my own wellbeing)
- feeling fulfilled by what I created
- spending time doing something I enjoyed
- overcoming creative blocks and experiencing a sense of achievement
- learning new things about myself
- helping other people by sharing my stories; and
- growing in self-confidence.

Creative activities can offer us so much – and all we really need to give them is a bit of time.

Finding intrinsic motivation in modern life

Being creative and engaging in hobbies is even more important in modern life than you might imagine. In societies where we are conditioned to highly value materialistic things – the latest gadgets, trendy clothing, bigger houses, fancier cars, and so on – we have become more focused on working to gain this stuff, rather than seeking out fun in everyday life. We are bombarded with advertisements and we feel compelled to keep up, rather than feel encouraged to find out what makes us genuinely happy.

By seeking to fulfil extrinsic goals (otherwise known as outward goals) such as financial success and status, we have shifted away from our intrinsic goals, like personal growth, relationships with ourselves and others, engaging in hobbies for pleasure, making the world a better place and the pursuit of knowledge (just for the fun of it).

However, numerous studies have found that the more we focus on material things and extrinsic goals, the less joyful we actually feel. Tim Kasser is an American psychologist who has spent years researching materialistic values and how they impact our lives. He's found that the more we focus on extrinsic goals, the lower our personal wellbeing, the less we behave well in social situations and the more our lifestyles tend to have a negative impact on the world.[1]

While these are all important findings, I want to repeat one in particular: the more we focus on extrinsic goals, the lower our personal wellbeing becomes. Or, in other words, the more we work to gain external things, the less happy, healthy and connected we are in everyday life.

Maybe you've even experienced this for yourself. Have you ever wanted a material thing so badly, only to obtain it and quickly lose interest, or start focusing on the next thing you want to get? Did you experience a sense of anticlimax, or emptiness, or even disappointment? The brief gratification of achieving your extrinsic goal didn't actually bring you genuine joy and instead left you needing more.

So, you may be wondering, if all the things we've been told will make us happy don't actually make us happy, then what does?

Here's one possible answer: the pursuit of intrinsic goals.

An intrinsic goal revolves around the journey of the goal, rather than the outcome. It connects you with activities that you're passionate about and which enable a sense of growth and expansion. Intrinsic goals also meet some of your core human needs, such as connection with yourself and others, physical health and contribution to society. You'll likely feel excited about your goal, not just for external reasons, but because it's truly meaningful to you.

Here are some examples of extrinsic and intrinsic goals, to help you understand the difference. Perhaps you can even reframe some of your own extrinsic goals to help you focus more on the potential intrinsic aspects of them!

EXTRINSIC	INTRINSIC
Practising yoga to achieve a certain pose, so you can share it on Instagram and get lots of likes.	Practising yoga because it makes you feel good.
Studying to achieve a certain grade.	Studying a topic that genuinely interests you.
Creating a blog because you want to become famous.	Creating a blog because you'd like to be creative and share your knowledge with others.
Playing music so you can make an album and get paid.	Playing music with your family because it brings you all together.

Something important to note is that having an extrinsic goal isn't a bad thing. There's nothing wrong with wanting to get paid, or trying to achieve a certain grade. However, if you can learn to focus on the intrinsic aspects of your goals more, then you may just find yourself feeling more fulfilled by them. Also, you might even achieve the extrinsic parts of your goals as a by-product of focusing on the intrinsic! For example, a study published in 2013 found that a group of 341 Iranian high-school students who were intrinsically motivated to study were both happier and achieved higher grades than their peers.[2] So not only were they more likely to enjoy the journey of their goals, but they performed better, too.

It's time to make a change in the way we live our everyday lives, with less focus on material gains and more effort going into our hobbies, creative activities, personal growth, connection and fun. If we can find a way to love what we do, not because we want to get something at the end of it, but because we can see the purpose and meaning behind it, then we are likely to become happier, more fulfilled and successful human beings.

Creativity and mindfulness

One of the brilliant things about creativity is that it can bring us into the present moment in a really powerful way. I've watched my boyfriend create amazing drawings and my mum crochet a blanket from scratch and my young cousins build towns out of Lego. In all of these different instances, it was clear just how present all of these people were. It was like seeing mindfulness in action, without anyone even trying! I believe this is the gift of creativity.

We can lose ourselves in the moment of creation, be it a painting, a photograph, or coffee art. It's not about trying to be mindful, it's simply allowing the creative process to unfold and learning to navigate judgements so we can immerse ourselves in the experience.

However, there may be more than mindfulness at play here.

Hungarian–American psychologist Mihaly Csikszentmihalyi, in 1990, named the psychological concept of flow: the enjoyable experience of being so immersed in an activity that nothing else seems to matter.[3] During flow, our senses, thoughts and feelings are all focused on the task at hand and we find balance between being challenged and enjoying what we're doing.

The key components of being in flow, as found by Csikszentmihalyi and his team, include:

- being totally focused and concentrating on the activity
- experiencing effortlessness, ecstasy and ease
- having great inner clarity by knowing what needs to be done and recognising how well you're doing
- believing in your ability to complete the activity; experiencing a balance between challenge and skills
- letting go of external concerns and distractions and losing self-conscious rumination
- being immersed in the present moment; losing your sense of time
- having intrinsic motivation because the activity is enjoyable, no matter the outcome.

In his TED talk, Csikszentmihalyi not only shared these key components of flow, but he also called flow experiences 'the secret to happiness'. If material things and extrinsic values are extinguishing our joy in everyday life, then creativity, flow and mindfulness may be the flames to light it up again.

When we engage in creative activities regularly, we open ourselves up to opportunities for mindfulness and flow. I believe this is one of the reasons why mindful colouring became so quickly popular and why it's now a beloved creative activity for many people. One of the key components of flow is having the skills to complete the task and while there are various creative activities that can help us find the state of flow, mindful colouring is one that many of us already have the skills for.

However, there may be a creative activity you already love doing (or have enjoyed in the past) that you could schedule regularly into your life. If you're feeling stuck or unsure, stay tuned for the next chapter, which will share a huge range of creative activities and ideas!

Claudia's story

Due to her medical condition, which involves not being able to engage in any form of physical exercise for an indefinite amount of time and not being able to focus on complex tasks, Claudia began exploring mindful activities that she would be able to do.

'In the process of exploring mindful activities,' she told me, 'I rediscovered something that I'd loved as a child, but had somehow forgotten about – painting by numbers. There are lovely designs for adults and doing it helps me practise mindfulness and be present in the moment by using the different colours, mindfully cleaning the brushes and concentrating on painting in the designated areas. It helps me feel calm.'

Creativity and judgements

As a child, you may have enjoyed a huge range of creative activities. For me, some of my favourite things to do included playing piano, dancing, writing, making fairy houses in the garden, 'cooking' at the river (using blackberries, sticks and anything else we could find), drawing horses, setting up play stations (like a doll-dressing station and a painting station) for my younger siblings and being their teacher, pressing flowers and making my own perfumes. I even organised a puppet show based on the movie *Shrek*, and made paper puppets from scratch!

It was only as I became a teenager that I lost more and more of my interest in being creative. Life became busier and I focused on achieving, instead of doing things just for fun. It seemed a bit pointless to try something new, when it would take time and effort to do it well! Why draw a horse unless it was going to look perfect? Why pretend being a teacher, or a banker, or a puppeteer when I was planning to be something else?

And so, the judgements started.

That's stupid. I'm no good. It's too hard. I hate this. I'm useless.
I'm not talented. It's pointless. Everything I make looks bad anyway.
When I try something new, I take too long to improve. This is
a waste of time.

The louder the judgements became, the more I retreated from my creative activities and stuck within my comfort zone of things I was already 'good at'. And I won't lie; it felt safe. However, as you may already know after reading the first chapter about exploring outside comfort zones, it also felt stagnant there. I knew I was missing out on fun things in life just because my judgemental thoughts made me feel as though I wasn't good enough and as though I couldn't do anything new (unless I was fairly certain I'd be good at it!).

As my mindfulness practices grew, I began noticing my judgemental thoughts. I heard them, I acknowledged them, I thanked them for trying to keep me safe, and then I let them go. I tried something new and creative and the judgemental thoughts returned. Loudly. I let them go. And yet those thoughts kept coming back, time and time again.

When I do creative things today, I still have judgemental thoughts. I'll write a sentence and immediately delete it. I'll take photographs and pick out the little flaws. I'll try new recipes and decide I'm a terrible cook.

But that's all okay, because I can have judgemental thoughts and know that I can let them go. I can hear judgemental thoughts and not let them stop me from being creative. I can hear judgemental thoughts and gently challenge them with some self-compassion.

Don't let your own judgemental thoughts hold you back from fun, exciting and meaningful creative experiences. Mindfulness is about embracing the present moment with openness, curiosity and a willingness to see what's unfolding, without judgement. If the judgement comes, practise letting it go and you'll find your mindfulness practice strengthening whenever you engage in creative activities (and likely in other areas, too).

How to let go of judgements:

- Visualise the thought as a balloon and watch it float away.
- Draw your attention back to the present moment by tuning in to one of your senses.
- Say to yourself: 'Thank you, but I don't need to believe this judgement right now.'
- Gently challenge the judgement with a positive thought or affirmation, such as 'Actually, I can just enjoy the process – I don't need to be perfect.'
- Show some self-compassion by acknowledging that you might be feeling nervous or intimidated and that your judgemental thoughts are only trying to save you from the situation (but that doesn't mean you need to believe them!).

CHAPTER 19

Hobbies and creative ideas

Rather than just giving you a list of creative activities to try, I thought I'd share some of my own experiences with different types of creativity. My hope is that by reading this chapter, you'll feel inspired and excited to be creative on your own, using one of my favourite creative activities or something else entirely!

I'd also like to encourage you to notice the way mindfulness is woven into each activity, with aspects of open-mindedness, curiosity, presence and nonjudgement. Identify when I've achieved states of 'flow' and start to think about how you could do this yourself, too.

Taking (and editing) flat-lay photos

It was a chilly day in Melbourne and the rain was coming down outside in a light but steady way. It was the perfect day to stay indoors and shoot flat-lay photos by choosing pretty or interesting items and photographing them from above. I found one of my favourite backdrops – a square board of wooden slats all nailed together (like a small section of fence) and laid it on the floor near a big window. I stood in front of my cupboard of flat-lay supplies, which I've slowly built up by purchasing things from op-shops and making decorations from scratch (like little plaster hearts and painted wooden spoons). I selected some of the decorations that I thought might work and scattered them around my flat-lay backdrop on the floor.

The light was perfect, so I decided not to set up my photography lights.

I placed all the items and decorations on the board and began moving them around. I tried to balance out the colours and sizes of the items, putting the big items diagonally across from each other and scattering everything else in-between.

I took a few photos and rearranged some things, trying new layouts and using a different colour palette. I even ducked outside in the rain to find a few autumn leaves to fill out some of the blank areas on the board.

Once I had a selection of photos to choose from, I realised nearly an hour had passed (while it had felt like twenty minutes!). I let the photos download onto my computer while I packed up everything.

After I'd finished packing up, I flicked through the photos and chose my favourite ones. I downloaded them into Lightroom (a photo-editing software) and applied some different presets (similar to filters) to find a nice look. I then adjusted a few more aspects, such as the exposure, shadows, white balance, contrast and saturation to make the colours pop and the whites brighter.

I had a deep sense of satisfaction and pride for what I'd created and I loved experimenting with my creativity and learning new things.

Organising an adventure

In late 2017, I organised a surprise trip to Tasmania for my partner's birthday. While the trip itself was incredible (so much so that we seriously considered moving there!), I found a huge amount of joy in creating the itinerary and organising the whole adventure.

I started with a blank Excel sheet (perhaps, not the most exciting way to kick off a creative activity, but bear with me).

I figured out the dates when we would visit and started searching online to find two different places to stay (one in Hobart and one in Launceston). I booked those, then added the accommodation information to the excel spreadsheet.

Once I knew where we would be, I started researching the areas and reading reviews of things to do. While it may not seem particularly creative, this is where I truly find a great sense of flow. I loved organising and thinking about the possibilities of an adventure and discovering hidden gems among the many articles about top things to do in Tasmania.

I found a two-hour group tour via boat, which would allow us to travel alongside the beautiful cliffs and watch seals playing (with the chance to see whales and dolphins, too!). After a bit of digging, I came across a rehabilitation centre for birds of prey, where we could attend a private tour and learn about some of the amazing birds in Tasmania. I read through various reviews of walks and found one that went to a large waterfall, passing natural caves along the way. Speaking of caves, I also found a few to visit that contained stalactites and stalagmites (and also, Australia's largest natural display of glow worms!).

The process of filtering through all the information and choosing beautiful, interesting and exciting adventures to fit into the trip was truly so engrossing for me. I was completely absorbed in the activity, feeling more and more satisfied with the choices I'd made and using creative ways of thinking to work everything out.

Guiding meditations

When I started studying my Advanced Certificate in Meditation, my skills in guiding meditation grew. I became comfortable creating meditations spontaneously and using my creativity to guide me (particularly during visualisations). I stopped planning everything I would say and let my imagination develop the experience, for both myself and others. I'll never forget the first time I relied solely on my creativity to guide me through improvising a visualisation meditation (which I was hosting live for someone else). I felt so much more free and trusting than I had when I was guiding meditations with a script. I could explore different colours, objects, scenery, emotions and ideas without knowing what would come next!

Perhaps the most powerful part of this type of creative activity was the ease with which I found myself letting go of all other thoughts and distractions. There was no need to try and focus on the present moment or bring my mind back when it wandered – I just felt captivated by the activity and how it was unfolding.

Mindful colouring

The first time I saw a mindful colouring book, I felt so excited about the concept. Not only is mindful colouring about being mindful and creative, it can be quite an easy activity to do.

However, the first few times I tried it, I couldn't find that state of flow. I felt so caught up in getting the colours right and worrying about going outside the lines and I couldn't stop thinking about the 'final product'. I wanted to finish colouring and have a gorgeous piece of artwork I could share on my social media accounts, but the whole process was taking so long, I couldn't imagine being able to actually finish an entire page! I felt frustrated and I started a heap of different pages in my colouring book, but never completed more than a quarter of any page.

Finally, I realised that I'd lost sight of the point of mindful colouring. It wasn't supposed to be about getting it 'right' or perfect, nor was it about the final product. Mindful colouring is about the journey and being allowed to experiment.

Once I let go of my own judgements, I found myself enjoying mindful colouring so much more and actually becoming absorbed in the creative activity. I realised that I didn't have to colour the leaves green and the sky blue. I could do whatever I wanted! And with that simple realisation, my creativity was able to take the reins and I began colouring just for the fun of it. I stopped wanting to share my colourings on social media and instead focused on colouring just for my own enjoyment. This was a really important lesson for me to learn; creating for others often takes away my carefree side because I become focused on making something perfect. When I can choose to create something for myself, then I can truly let my creativity take over and guide me however it likes.

Blogging

When I finished studying psychology, coaching and counselling at university, I had no idea what a blog was. I didn't know what I was going to do next in my life, but I did know I wanted to keep learning about mental health and help other people in some way. For a few months, I worked and waited for the next step in my life to become clear. After some research, I decided I should create a website, so that I could build a potential client base to work with. I started my blog when I didn't even really know what 'blog' meant, but it wasn't long before I was immersed in the world of it.

Once I started to find bloggers who had created incredible online businesses, I felt an incredible sense of purpose. I signed up for a blogging course and began to really understand the power of a blog. It had the potential to be a hub of helpful information and genuine stories and a space where people could go to feel inspired and supported, not to mention the fact that it could be accessed all over the world!

And for me, I saw an opportunity to create my own career, so that I could do what I loved and eventually earn an income from it.

With all that in mind, I quickly built a website and started posting articles about wellness. I built a small community of subscribers (people who signed up via email to receive my newsletters) and started a Facebook page. Over the course of six months, I realised that I wanted to blog more about mental health and psychology rather than wellbeing in general and I decided to deactivate my first blog and start all over again.

With the new blog, I hired a wonderful website developer and paid a designer to create a meaningful logo. I watched countless tutorials about how to continue building and designing the website myself, then rebranded another six months later. By that stage, my social media accounts and subscribers were growing quite quickly (also due to the fact that I'd started a podcast, which was regularly featured at the top of the iTunes charts).

I was creating daily and it felt like my creativity knew no bounds. If I wasn't writing, I was podcasting or taking photos for my articles and social media. I was regularly building new pages on my website and trying different ideas to see how I could reach more people.

In October 2016, I rebranded again, this time working closely with my partner to incorporate a new colour palette into my website along with a completely new layout. Having studied design and animation, he was also able to create beautiful graphics and help me take much nicer photos!

My blog continues to evolve regularly, but I love that about it. It's a creative outlet I turn to whenever I feel lost and it provides me with a platform to connect with others and find new creative opportunities. Just because it's my job, it doesn't mean that it can't be creative!

The challenge of creativity

One of the challenging things I find about creativity is its unpredictability. Some days, it flows easily, and on other days it seems more and more elusive. I've been challenged to let go of my perfectionist tendencies and to find purpose and enjoyment in creating, even when it doesn't go the way I planned. However, the unpredictability of creativity is also part of the fun! When I start something creative, I never know where it will take me or how the experience will unfold. Perhaps that's why it's so easy to be mindful when I'm being creative; it encourages me to let go of trying to control things and instead just let it flow.

When creative activities don't go to plan, it's also a wonderful opportunity to practise mindfulness. Rather than being self-critical and wishing I'd done things differently, I can try to appreciate the activity for the journey (rather than the outcome) and practise letting go of my judgements.

If I find myself getting caught up in thoughts like 'I'm so bad at this' or 'My creative activity was a waste of time' or 'I should have done something differently,' that's a great time to refocus on the present moment (perhaps using a breathing technique or by tuning into my senses). This allows me to gently let go of the thoughts and move my attention back to the present moment and I often realise that my thoughts were trying to create problems when there were none. So what if I coloured outside the lines in a colouring book? Or if my flat-lay photos were too dark or out of focus? Or if I had to rewrite an article because it didn't quite 'sound' right? It might be frustrating at times, but it's not the end of the world.

Now that I've shown you a few glimpses into my creative activities, I'd love for you to choose one and try it out yourself. If none of my activities particularly resonated with you, be sure to check out the list of more creative activities on the next page.

More creative ideas

- Make a raised garden bed
- Crochet a blanket
- Press flowers
- Use watercolour paints to paint flowers
- Redecorate your bedroom
- Write a novel
- Make bath salts or bath bombs
- Draw a comic strip
- Take photos of the night sky
- Play a musical instrument
- Make coconut yoghurt
- Do macramé
- Learn calligraphy
- Build a succulent garden
- Go dancing
- Arrange flowers
- Paint something completely abstract
- Make jewellery
- Brew ginger beer
- Learn how to animate short videos
- Create a DIY gift for someone you care about
- Bake a new cake recipe
- Write a letter to a friend
- Make a vision board
- Print a mandala and colour it in
- Create your own smoothie recipe
- Make a herb garden
- Build a cubby house or indoor fort
- Write a list of things you're grateful for.

Regular creative activities

I know how quickly excitement and inspiration can wear off. It might take a few seconds, it might take a few days or weeks, but eventually the initial motivation will start to fade. That's why it's really important to set up solid habits and make helpful plans so you can follow through on your good intentions, even when it might feel difficult. The more you can incorporate creative activities into your life, the more you'll have a chance to practise mindfulness and enjoy all the different aspects creativity has to offer.

Here's a simple way to set yourself up with a plan.

First of all, choose your favourite creative activities from this chapter and either highlight them or write them down on a piece of paper.

Break down the steps of the creative activities into smaller chunks. For example, to build a succulent garden you might need to:

- find a space in your existing garden
- do some research about how best to plant succulents and keep them alive
- buy succulents (or see if you can have a cutting from a friend's garden)
- plant the succulents
- maintain your new garden.

Grab your calendar or planner and write down the dates and times when you can implement the steps of the creative activities you've selected. For example, next Monday, you can find a space in your garden and research more about succulents from 5 pm until 6 pm. On Thursday between 4 pm and 6 pm, you can go to your friend's place to pick up the succulents she said you could have. You might plant the succulents in your garden on Saturday morning between 8 am and 10 am. Each day for the following week, you'll check on your succulent garden between

5.30 pm and 6 pm. Maybe you could even take some photos to share! After a while, you might like to rearrange your succulent garden, or add new things to it.

Once you feel satisfied with this creative activity and you have time for something new, you can choose the next activity on your list to try. Slowly but surely, your creative activities will become infused in your life and you'll have even more opportunities to be mindful regularly.

PART SEVEN

Mindful Social Media

CHAPTER 20

Mindful social media

Love it or loathe it, social media is here to stay. With millions of people connecting online and the rise of platforms that enable that connection, it's clear that social media has very quickly become an ingrained aspect of modern society. It allows us to explore new ideas, share our thoughts, express creativity, discover more about the world and be inspired by people we look up to. On a larger scale, social media has been used to create positive change and garner support for various causes, such as conservation, wildlife protection and education (to name just a few!).

In a relatively short amount of time, social media has also enabled businesses to thrive and created entirely new careers, from social media managers to travel influencers. It's taken just twenty years to build social media into what it currently is today and, quite honestly, this idea blows me away. Social media is incredibly powerful, that much is obvious.

However, the various negative impacts of social media are also clear to be seen. The average person currently spends almost two hours on social media each day, adding up to fourteen hours every week and more than five years over the average lifespan. With social media constantly evolving to become more addictive, exciting, interactive and accessible, I can imagine that these numbers will easily increase.

Since social media is still relatively new, we have no real idea what the long-term ramifications could be, but initial findings are already pointing towards higher levels of anxiety and depression, and greater exposure to bullying and distressing content. In terms of physical health, numerous studies have shown that people regularly using their phones tend to develop unhealthy postures, resulting in neck and back pain. The bright light of phones can be damaging for our eyes, potentially leading to macular degeneration and worsening eyesight. Phone light can also impact our sleep, tricking the body into thinking it's still daylight and delaying the release of melatonin (a hormone which helps us fall asleep). Not to mention the possible increase of sedentary activities to accommodate the time we spend on our phones!

The good news is you get to choose how much you actually engage in social media use. It is your responsibility to choose when, why and how you use it, and in this chapter I'll show you how to simplify and enhance your social media use, as well as effectively decrease the time you spend mindlessly on social media.

Simplifying social media use

Snapchat, Facebook, Instagram, Twitter, Pinterest, Tumblr, WhatsApp, QQ, Skype, Viber, Myspace (remember that?!). It's no wonder we end up spending so much time on social media with multiple platforms right at our fingertips.

One of the easiest ways to cut that time down is just to simplify what you use and how you use it.

A few years ago, I had more social media accounts than I had time for. I couldn't keep up with them all and it felt incredibly overwhelming and frustrating. I had just launched my business and I was trying to grow my communities, hoping to reach people who would benefit from my work in mindfulness and stress management. Every time I saw new growth, I felt a rush of excitement and happiness and before long I was hooked on the numbers. My social media use became less about the people who were following me and more about myself. I knew it didn't feel right, but I wasn't really sure where I'd gone wrong.

I was trying to implement all the tips I'd read about growing an audience: posting daily at the same time, being consistent, interacting with people who might want to follow me, trying to keep up with all the comments and private messages on the different platforms, taking quality photos, sharing funny and insightful posts (with helpful information as well), waking up early and checking my phone straightaway, checking my phone before I fell asleep, and worrying about not being on social media when I couldn't be on it.

I wasn't enjoying it and I could tell I was focusing on aspects of social media that weren't meaningful or fulfilling. I didn't want to feel compelled to check my phone all the time and I also didn't want it to interfere with the rest of my life. And so I made some changes. Not only did these changes help me let go of the frustration and stress I was feeling, they also enabled me to find my way back to enjoying some of the benefits social media has to offer: connection, creativity and making a difference.

Here are my three top tips for not being overwhelmed by social media.

1: Delete social media accounts you don't need

I thought about deleting my Twitter account for several months before I actually did it. I worried that my followers would be angry with me and that less people would find my website and that I'd miss out on potential growth. When I made the decision and deactivated the account, I was surprised to find that nothing happened.

Nothing at all.

And I realised that it didn't really matter. It didn't matter if I wasn't posting every day, it didn't matter if I wasn't 'following the rules' for growth, it didn't even matter if I deleted an entire account!

Suddenly, I freed up both the space in my mind I'd been using to worry about Twitter and the time I normally spent on it (that I didn't even enjoy). I felt less scattered, less overwhelmed and more empowered.

Take a moment to think about the social media platforms you currently use. Do they add meaning, value or inspiration to your life? Or do they tend to drain your energy and create stress? Try deactivating any accounts that you feel ready to let go of (even if just for a short while) and notice how it feels.

Then use the time you would have spent on that social media account to practise mindfulness, engage in self-care, go for a walk, spend time with the people you care about, read a book or start a new hobby!

2: Create intentions for your social media use

My intentions when I use Instagram are to express my creativity and connect with people. My intention when I use Facebook is to share helpful information. My intention when I use my personal Pinterest account is to collect inspiration for travelling, DIY projects and photography. My intention when I use my business Pinterest account is to send traffic to my website.

Those are my honest and most meaningful intentions for using the different social media platforms I currently engage in. I am very clear about what I use social media for, which makes it so much simpler and less overwhelming. I know exactly what my goal is when I open up a platform and how I can best use the time I spend there.

What are your intentions when you use social media?

Can you connect with your intention before you even open up a platform and recognise when you're no longer fulfilling that intention?

3: Take regular social media detoxes

Taking deliberate time off your phone and away from social media can help break the habits that form when you consistently use social media. It also gives you a chance to re-evaluate and reflect on how social media may be impacting on, or interfering with, your life. I've personally found that doing regular social media detoxes feels refreshing, liberating and proactive, and I enjoy having time without my phone glued to my side.

You might like to start by taking a break for an hour from social media at a time when you might normally be using it.

Then you can increase that time to a few hours, perhaps a day, a weekend, a whole week. Try to only use your phone when necessary – and delete social media apps if you need to! This won't delete your entire account (just whether or not it appears on your phone) and you can always download them again later.

One lesson I learned during my first social media detox was just how much my mind would try to convince me to use it. Even though I wasn't using social media on my phone, I found myself logging in via my computer or asking my partner to check my accounts for me! Be aware that it's not always easy to take a break from habits that have become ingrained and feel compelling. If you find yourself struggling, show yourself gentle compassion, learn any lessons you might need to learn and just keep trying. Remember that taking some time away from social media won't mean the end of the world, your relationships won't break down, you won't lose all your followers or friends, you'll be able to catch up on things later and you deserve to spend some meaningful time in the real world, not just the digital one.

Enhancing your experiences with social media

I can't even begin to tell you how many wonderful experiences I've had because of social media. I've visited beautiful places because I saw someone else's post about it, I've taught mindfulness to people all over the world, I've discovered a passion for photography, I've earned money from a post, I've been inspired during difficult times and I've made real and lasting friendships.

By learning to use social media in positive ways, I've added value to my life and experienced some real benefits. And you can, too! Here's how.

Connect with people

Use social media to discover people you admire, connect with your friends and loved ones, offer kindness and compassion, meet new people with similar interests and engage in meaningful interactions. You'll discover more about this in the next chapter.

Put 'real life' first

There was a phase I went through several years ago of photographing my food and coffee when I visited cafés, so I could post them on Instagram. It wasn't long before I realised that by doing this, I was interfering with the quality time I could be spending with whoever I was with at the time.

Similarly, while on a beautiful adventure in another country, I realised that I was more concerned about getting the 'perfect photo' than appreciating the actual experience.

Even though I enjoy taking photos and sharing them, I now make a conscious effort to put my real life first. It's more important to me to experience and savour the moment than to simply capture the image of it.

You might like to explore doing this yourself by deliberately putting your phone away and just sinking into the experience, without distractions. For example, would you rather wake up in the morning and quickly check Instagram to see how many people liked your photo from the night before, or practise mindfulness by slowly stretching your body and feeling a sense of gratitude for the warmth and comfort of your bed? Would you rather take an Instagram story (or Snapchat video or Facebook live) of your pet playing outside, or go out there and actually play with him? Would you rather snap photos of your food, or eat it while it's still warm? These are all questions I still ask myself regularly to identify whether the present moment would be more special and meaningful without social media.

Find inspiration

There are many thousands of talented people on social media. Photographers, decor stylists, chefs, fashion bloggers, writers, architects, travel influencers, watercolour painters, videographers, gardeners … You can find talented people doing amazing things in just about every field or niche you can think of!

Look at some of your own interests and passions and discover people on social media who can inspire and motivate you. There are many people now teaching their knowledge and skills to help people just like you, who want to learn more. It's an incredible advantage of media in the modern world and creates so much opportunity for growth!

Try looking for groups or searching for hashtags that relate to the area you're interested in. You can find articles on Pinterest, behind-the-scenes videos on Instagram, tutorials on YouTube, groups on Facebook and a range of other exciting methods for learning. Take some time to actively explore and discover and you'll quickly find some of the positivity social media has to offer!

Be mindful

If there was ever a place to find a whole lot of judgement, it's social media. Read through the comments on just one popular photo and you'll likely see trolling behaviour, criticisms, verbal attacks and arguments. Perhaps it's the feeling of invincibility which comes from commenting via a screen rather than face to face, or having access to such a wide range of people with diverse beliefs and ideas, or the tendency to forget that other 'users' of social media are real people, too. Social media is incredibly rife with judgement.

In my opinion, this makes it a great place to practise nonjudgement (one of the important aspects of your mindfulness practice). The more you can learn to be open-minded, accepting and understanding on social media, the more it will translate into your real life.

Notice when images or words have triggered judgemental thoughts and see if you can explore letting them go.

For example, rather than judging a photo of a person on social media as ugly, undeserving or boring (or any other kind of judgement), practise just observing what you see, accepting that other people may be different from you and moving on.

Explore your feelings

You can learn a great deal about yourself by exploring your emotional reactions to posts on social media. Create the space to compassionately and nonjudgementally observe your feelings by asking yourself some simple questions in an effort to understand more about why you might be feeling the way you do.

Some questions might include:

- Do I feel jealous?
- Am I upset because I have different core values from what was posted?
- Does the post remind me of a negative experience?
- Do I have some irrational beliefs to work through?

Once you've acknowledged what you're feeling, ask yourself:

- What do I need to support myself through this emotional response?

You might like to talk to someone about it, do a social media detox, practise mindfulness, or engage in self-care.

Strategies to decrease mindless social media use

This chapter wouldn't be complete without some helpful tips on how to decrease mindless social media use! I encourage you to choose one of the tips below and start implementing it today. Continue using the tip for a full week and then take some time to reflect on what you noticed. Did anything surprise you? Did you feel resistance, or struggle to implement the tip for any particular reason? Did you learn anything about yourself?

Then next week, try another one of the tips and repeat the reflection process.

Once you've tried all the tips, explore what worked well for you and implement them in the ways that best resonate with you. As this unfolds, you might even discover your own helpful methods of decreasing the amount of time you mindlessly use social media!

Set a timer

When I spend time on social media, it feels like seconds have passed when it's actually been several minutes. It *always* surprises me how quickly time passes without me even noticing! To help myself become used to spending shorter amounts of time on social media, I started setting a timer. It worked really well because it helped me actually choose how much time I wanted to dedicate to social media and not go over that amount of time (which I was very prone to doing before).

Try setting your own timer and be strict with yourself about closing down your social media when the timer goes off. No 'five more minutes!' or 'just ten more posts' or 'just one more article!' If it's important enough, you can always return to it later.

Know your patterns and triggers

Do you tend to open social media when you're bored? Or when you're tired? Maybe you prefer to use social media when you're procrastinating over something important. Perhaps it's a time-filler during your breaks at work.

Know and understand your own patterns and triggers so you can be more intentional with your time.

For example, I used to always jump on social media, particularly Instagram, when I was taking a bath. Even though it was meant to be a self-caring, relaxing and rejuvenating activity, I'd take my phone with me and scroll through Instagram until the water went cold – and then I'd feel disappointed because I didn't properly appreciate taking a bath! Once I recognised this pattern, I decided to start leaving my phone out of the bathroom so that I could enjoy a relaxing bath.

Don't go down the rabbit hole of clicking links

One minute, you're scrolling through Instagram and the next, you've clicked a link to a blog article. From the blog article, you discover a video (which you spend fifteen minutes watching), then another video gets suggested for you, so you start to watch that, too. In the second video, you hear about a beautiful Instagram account, so you head over there to check it out. Around and around it goes and suddenly it's half an hour later, you're on a completely random YouTube channel and you can't even remember how (or why) you got there.

Try to get into the habit of just using one social media platform at a time – and if you absolutely must click a link elsewhere, make the decision to read or watch whatever is at the end of that link and then switch your phone off afterwards.

Use mindfulness instead

It's more common in today's society to see people waiting and looking at their phones than to see people just waiting. I was in a queue at the grocery store recently and every single person in the queue was using their phone. The last time I caught the train, there were more people looking down at their devices than watching the sunrise. If you go walking through a shopping centre, I can almost guarantee that the people waiting outside shops (perhaps while their partner is buying something) will be on their phones. This is the media-driven world that we live in. It's fast-paced, constantly changing and no one wants to miss anything.

However, using mindfulness instead of going on your phone can be a great way to not only decrease mindless social media to use, but to add more mindfulness into your everyday life.

Next time you're waiting (for a friend, in a queue, at a café, on public transport, or wherever else), put your phone away and tune in to your breath. Notice the feeling of each breath moving in and out of your body. Pay attention to the rise and fall of your chest and belly. Explore what each breath feels like inside your nostrils. Just take a few moments to breathe mindfully and enjoy some time of calm and relaxation.

CHAPTER 21

Creating meaningful connections through social media

When it comes to social media, I have a lot to be thankful for. I've made new friends, reconnected with family members I hadn't seen in years, joined inspiring communities and used the wisdom of the people I admire to try different things in my own life. There are so many wonderful things which have come to fruition simply because I've tried to become more intentional, mindful and genuine in my relationships via social media. It can get a bad rap, but if it is used cleverly, social media can be a great facilitator of meaningful connections. In this chapter, I'll share some of the ways you can connect with others and also some ideas for using social media to your advantage.

Strengthening relationships

Reconnecting with family

One day on Facebook I found my great-uncle; more than ten years had passed since the last time I'd seen him. It turned out we'd actually been living in the same city for a few years without even knowing! Because of Facebook, we had the opportunity to organise a catch-up in person and we've since spent hours chatting, eating good food together (he is an incredible baker) and going for walks.

When we use it to connect with other people, social media can have such a powerful and positive influence. It provides a safe and easy space to get in touch and possibly even organise in-person meet-ups. At the same time, even if you live on the other side of the world to your friends and family, social media can still help you stay connected with one another.

Action tip: Browse through the 'Friends' section of your Facebook account and find someone in your family you haven't spoken with in a while. Send them a thoughtful message to ask how they're going and, if it feels natural, allow a conversation to flow from there.

Staying in touch with friends

When I moved to the city, I lost contact with many of my friends from home. City life was hectic, I felt particularly introverted, I was getting used to living in my own place – and when I did go back home, I spent time with my family. Over the years, I've stayed in touch with my friends via social media, which has allowed us to share our journeys with each other and catch up when we get the chance.

Tips for using social media

Be an 'active' rather than a 'passive' friend on social media. When one of your friends posts something, don't just like it and scroll on. Instead, take a little bit of time to leave a thoughtful comment and let your friend know you care.

Be mindful of who you are following. It's easy to follow many friends, brands, strangers, celebrities and businesses on social media, but the more you follow, the less you are likely to see posts that are actually meaningful to you. While social media algorithms are becoming more sophisticated and try to guess which posts you would prefer to see, they won't always get it right and the posts you actually want to engage with will be lost. To stop this from happening too often, start unfollowing anyone you don't actually want or need to be following. When I went through the list of Instagram accounts I was keeping up with, I found many I didn't really want to continue following – cafés I'd been to once, clothing brands I didn't wear any more, people I didn't know at all and celebrities I didn't feel the particular need to see on my feed. When I stopped following them, it freed up more space in my feed for people I really cared about and gave me more opportunities to connect with them.

Asking for support

Not only does social media provide the opportunity to interact with people regularly, it also creates the potential to ask for support when it's needed. I've seen countless examples of people going through difficult times – suffering the loss of a loved one, experiencing illness (both mental and physical), going through a break-up, or facing challenges as a new parent – who have reached out to their circle and then received meaningful support.

In many cases, I think some people actually find it easier to ask for help online than in person. Perhaps it feels less confronting to type a request for support than to speak the words out loud. Or maybe there's more chance of receiving validation and understanding when there are more people listening to what you need to say.

However, it can be important to remember that being vulnerable online also opens you up to people who might not be particularly kind, supportive or understanding. Whenever I post something, I first ask myself if it's something I truly feel ready to share. If not, I'll often find someone to talk with in person before I share anything online.

Action tip: Next time you would like to hear some advice or ask for support, share a post on social media and see what your friends might have to say. It doesn't necessarily have to be something incredibly important – it could be something simple like recommendations about where to go on holiday or tips for dealing with stress.

Meeting new people

Discovering like-minded people

It's not always easy to find new people you naturally click with. When I finished studying at university but continued working at the same place I'd been at for the previous few years, I noticed my social life stagnated a bit (actually, quite a lot!). However, I also enrolled in an online course that allowed me to become part of an exclusive Facebook group. Within this group, I met many people I had heaps in common with: we were creating blogs, we were interested in wellness and mental health, and we were also growing our small businesses for the purposes of helping others and working in a way we enjoyed.

Many of these people I've become close friends with and we've shared some really wonderful times over the years. In fact, I have even collaborated with quite a few of them in different ways, via interviews and workshops.

Action tip: Do some research to find hashtags that are particularly relevant for you. I often search for posts that use hashtags related to blogging, flat-lay photography, meditation and Cavalier King Charles spaniels. Before I travel to new destinations, I like to browse through relevant hashtags to discover the best places to visit, such as great cafés and pretty landscapes, and to search for local tips. For example, when I was planning a trip to Tasmania, I browsed through the hashtags #hobartandbeyond and #discovertasmania (to name a few!).

So what are your interests in life? What inspires you? What would you like to learn? Once you have a few ideas, just type the hashtags into the search section of whichever social media platform you might be using and enjoy!

Not long after we welcomed our second Cavalier King Charles puppy into our family, I started a new Instagram account for her and her older brother. The original intention for their account was to keep our close family updated with their growth, but Moose and Minnie quickly gained followers from around the world. One day, I received a message from another dog owner in Melbourne, who invited us to a monthly walk just for Cavalier King Charles spaniels and their owners! It still amazes me how many opportunities I've found (or received) as a result of being on social media.

After my mum joined Instagram, she had a similar experience as a result of sharing photos of her beautiful garden. She began connecting with other gardeners and even visited some in person! Not only did she meet like-minded people, but she started discovering more ideas and inspiration that she could incorporate into her own garden. Instagram became a source of connection and inspiration for her and I was excited to see it all unfold.

Having a sense of community

Even though I was only just learning how to create flat-lay photos, I felt both welcomed and inspired by a creative online community called Creatively Squared. By using their specific hashtags, my photos were shared with the creators and members of their community, many of whom encouraged me, offered helpful advice and answered my questions about how to improve my photos. Having that sense of community helped me persevere and created a supportive space for me to learn and feel included.

Action tip: There are many, many Facebook groups that can offer a brilliant sense of community and inclusiveness. I'm a member of a Facebook group book club, a few groups about business and a few groups about wellness. They're a great place to find support, connect with like-minded people, share things you've learned and feel that sense of community. Take the time to find some Facebook groups you could join and put in the effort to connect with other people in there.

Connecting with people who can inspire you

Learning from others

Did you know that many podcasters have their own Facebook groups for their listeners to join? And there are online courses that offer Facebook groups so you can continue learning with other people who also enrolled in the course?

With the growing popularity of live video, more and more people are sharing helpful knowledge and experiences with their followers – often for free!

Social media can offer fantastic opportunities that allow you to learn from other people and gain new knowledge and skills.

Action Tip: Think about the people you would most like to learn from and then search on social media to find if they have any accounts. Follow them for a while to discover if they'll offer helpful posts, live videos, or groups.

Finding new opportunities

In 2017, I became a writer for a wonderful online platform simply because I saw a Facebook post about an open position on their team. A few years before, when I'd first discovered that platform, I actually wrote on my vision board that I wanted to submit an article for them to publish. I submitted an article and felt absolutely over the moon when they agreed to share it.

I never imagined that I would become a regular writer on their team (getting paid to do something I really loved), but thanks to social media, that was exactly what happened. New opportunities pop up on social media in various ways – some people are literally making a living from posting on their social media accounts by working with brands they resonate with.

However, opportunities on social media don't always have to revolve around making money. It can also be used a powerful force for sharing messages and pushing for positive change. Many people with large followings are using their influence to support causes they believe in. I've signed petitions, donated to charities and used my own voice to share messages so I can play my own part in creating positive change, no matter how small.

Seeing new things and discovering different possibilities

It may be true that people tend to post their 'highlight reels' on social media. Basically, we see the best moments of everyone else's lives and this can lead us to believe that they all wear beautiful clothes, do fun activities, go to incredible places and enjoy delicious food regularly. We compare our 'behind the scenes' with other people's 'highlight reels' and end up feeling not good enough.

Not to mention the fact that people who gain large followings are often able to invest in hiring professional photographers, getting their hair and makeup done and having their photos edited to perfection. However, those flawless photos don't always tell the whole story!

I remember one particular time when I saw a photo on Pinterest of someone reading on their bed with their legs up the wall and I thought it looked so cool that I tried to replicate it. I even painted my toenails red (I think it might have been the only time I'd painted my toenails in a few years!). I also put on a pair of nice jeans, which I would never have normally relaxed in because they were quite tight. I climbed on the bed and lay down with my legs up the wall (which took a bit of manoeuvring, thanks to my jeans) and Moose jumped up on the bed with me and started rolling and jumping around. My partner probably took about fifty photos. Maybe more. As soon as we were finished taking photos, I climbed off the bed and put my tracksuit pants back on.

Just by the way, it's super uncomfortable to lie with your legs up the wall while reading a book! The book was heavy, my legs got pins and needles and I couldn't even read because the light was shining in my eyes. Anyway, I chose the best photo – one where Moose actually settled down for a few seconds next to me – and posted it. It received some lovely comments and I felt glad to have created a photo I was proud of.

But that's the thing; I *created* the photo. It wasn't a quick snapshot of a natural moment in my life.

It can be really important to remember that what gets posted online is not usually the whole story. It's common for people to select the images which look the best or tell the best story. Even natural-looking photos don't always reflect what's really going on for someone. I can take a pretty photo of flowers and create an inspirational post when I'm feeling stressed or sad. I can share a cute photo of my dogs cuddling together when they actually only stayed there for a few seconds before getting annoyed with each other. I've created flat-lay photos with tea that didn't get drunk because it cooled down while I was taking photos of it.

However, social media does allow you to discover new possibilities and exposes you to things you may not have ever known without it. I've been inspired to try interesting recipes and do my hair in different ways. I've seen stunning landscapes which are now on my list of places to visit. I've discovered new music, new styles of photography, new quotes, new books, new movies. Social media is like an ever-evolving advertisement for things to try and learn, but the difference is we get to largely control what we see (and don't see).

For example, when I first started my Instagram account, I followed many yoga and food pages because those were topics I was interested in and wanted to incorporate more into my own life. As my interests changed, so did the accounts that I followed. These days, I tend to follow accounts that feature flat-lay and landscape photography, beautiful travel accounts and small business accounts that inspire me to try new things in my own business.

Final thoughts on connections and social media

Among the billions of people using social media, not everyone has the best intentions. While social media can be a fantastic way to connect with people and share things that are important to you, it's also imperative that you keep yourself safe. Unless you 100 per cent know and trust every person who follows you, don't share your home address, identifying information, or anything else you wouldn't want a stranger to know.

Unfortunately, bullying, trolling and nasty comments have been on the rise. Protect your own wellbeing by blocking anything that doesn't serve you, and talk to someone who can help if you don't know what to do.

Guidelines for social media

- Be kind and supportive: treat other people the way you want to be treated.
- Set boundaries: don't go on social media when you're having a bad day.
- Allow others to have a voice: you won't agree with everyone online, and that's okay.
- Block hate: don't bother arguing with trolls – just block and move on.
- Seek help: in the event that you're being bullied online (or feeling upset about something you've read or seen), talk to someone who can support you and provide guidance on what to do next.

One last word

As the philosopher Lao-Tzu once said, 'The journey of a thousand miles begins with a single step.' Flick back to your favourite chapter of this book and choose one tip or mindfulness technique you could implement today. Then do the same tomorrow. Slowly, but surely, mindfulness can become a natural part of your everyday routine and perhaps even a foundation upon which you build a more intentional, present and open-minded life.

I hope that you can return to this book whenever you need inspiration or support and guidance. It's normal to feel a little lost sometimes, or to readjust your mindfulness practices to suit new changes. You may like to experiment with new ways of mindful living and discover different methods of practising mindfulness.

This isn't a journey to be rushed or criticised. It's a journey to savour and experiment with. Mindfulness isn't always about being serious, calm and steadfast; try having fun with your practice! Implement new meditation techniques or make up your own, keep learning, encourage a friend or family member to attend a yoga or meditation class with you, read more books about mindfulness and experiment with self-care.

More than anything, don't be afraid of being unique. Your mindfulness practice is an expression of your lifestyle, personality, attitude, passions, goals and beliefs. Allow it to be authentic and you'll soon find your mindfulness practice becoming an important aspect of who you are and how you live your life.

Thank you for being one of The Mindful Kind.

With love,

Rach

References and Further Reading

Chapter 1

1. Robert Yerkes & John Dodson, 'The Relation of Strength of Stimulus to Rapidity of Habit-Formation', *Journal of Comparative Neurology & Psychology*, 1908, no. 18, pp. 459–482.

Chapter 2

1. E.A. Hoge et al., 'Randomized control trial of mindfulness meditation for generalized anxiety disorder: effects on anxiety and stress reactivity', *Journal of Clinical Psychiatry*, August 2013, vol. 74, no. 8, pp. 786–792.
2. F. Zeidan, S.K. Johnson, B.J. Diamond, Z. David & P. Goolkasian, 'Mindfulness meditation improves cognition: evidence of brief mindfulness training', *Consciousness and Cognition*, June 2010, vol. 19, no. 2, pp. 597–605.
3. Willem Kuyken et al., 'Effectiveness and cost-effectiveness of mindfulness-based cognitive therapy compared with maintenance antidepressant treatment in the prevention of depressive relapse or recurrence (PREVENT): A randomised control trial', *The Lancet*, 4 July 2015, vol. 386, no. 9988, pp. 63–73.

Chapter 4

1. M. Gazzaniga, T. Heatherton & D. Halpern, Psychological Science, 2010, W.W. Norton & Company, New York, pp. 414–415.
2. *ibid*, pp. 414–415.
3. *ibid*, pp. 414–415.

Chapter 6

1. A. Levine & R. Heller, *Attached*, Tarcher, 2010.
2. J.M. Gottman & R.W. Levenson, 'Marital processes predictive of later dissolution: behaviour, physiology, and health', *Journal of Personality and Social Psychology*, 1992.

Chapter 10

1. Delwyn Bartlett, 'Managing Insomnia: What we've learned in the last 10 years', *InPsych*, Australian Psychological Society, April 2014, vol. 36, issue 2.

Chapter 12

1. P. Martinez-Lozano Sinues, M. Kohler & R. Zenobi, 'Human breath analysis may support the existence of individual metabolic phenotypes', *PLoS* ONE, 2013, vol. 8, no. 4.
2. Russ Harris, *The Happiness Trap*, Trumpeter, 2008.

Chapter 13

1. P. Kini, J. Wong, S. McInnis, N. Gabana & J.W. Brown, 'The effects of gratitude expression on neural activity', *NeuroImage*, March 2016, vol. 128, pp. 1–10.

Chapter 14

1. G. Mark, D. Gudith & U. Klocke, 'The Cost of Interrupted Work: More Speed and Stress', CHI 2008 Conference on Human Factors in Computing Systems – Proceedings, 2008, pp. 107–110.

2. E.H. Kozasa et al. 'Meditation training increases brain efficiency in an attention task', *NeuroImage*, 2 January 2012, vol. 59, no. 1, pp. 745–749.

3. E.R. Valentine & P.L.G. Sweet, 'Meditation and attention: A comparison of the effects of concentrative and mindfulness meditation on sustained attention', *Mental Health, Religion & Culture*, 1999, vol. 2, no. 1, pp. 59–70.

Chapter 16

1. M. An, S. Colarelli, K. O'Brien & M.E. Boyajian, 'Why We Need More Nature at Work: Effects of Natural Elements and Sunlight on Employee Mental Health and Work Attitudes', *PLoS* ONE, 23 May 2016, vol. 11, no. 5.

Chapter 17

1. Elizabeth Gilbert, *Big Magic*, Bloomsbury Publishing, London, 2015.

2. B. Fisher & D. Specht, 'Successful Aging and Creativity in Later Life', *Journal of Aging Studies*, 1999, vol. 13, no. 4, pp 457–472.

3. High blood pressure statistics, Heart Foundation, https://www.heartfoundation.org.au/about-us/what-we-do/heart-disease-in-australia/high-blood-pressure-statistics (accessed online 3 December 2018).

4. *Chef's Table*, Netflix, 2016, Season 2, Episode 2.

Chapter 18

1. Tim Kasser interview on *The True Cost* website, https://truecostmovie.com/tim-kasser-interview/ (accessed online 3 December 2018).

2. A. Khoshnam, M. Ghamari & A.G. Gendavani, 'The Relationship Between Intrinsic Motivation and Happiness with Academic Achievement in High School Students', *International Journal of Academic Research in Business and Social Sciences, November 2013, vol. 3, no. 11,* pp. 330–336.

3. Mihaly Csikszentmihalyi, 'Flow: The Psychology of Optimal Experience', *Journal of Leisure Research*, January 1990, vol. 24, no. 1, pp. 93–94.

Acknowledgements

This book wouldn't be in your hands right now if it weren't for some truly wonderful people.

Thank you to Katie from ABC Books and HarperCollins for sending me the email that kickstarted the incredible adventure of writing a book.

I'd like to send a huge amount of gratitude to Helen, Madeleine and Rachel for their amazing skills in managing and editing this book and for creating the cover for *The Mindful Kind*. I so appreciate all your time and effort and for being so gentle with this first-time author!

I had a dedicated team of people who were more than happy to proofread chapters and share kind feedback: my beautiful mum, my wonderful friend Alyse and my boyfriend (now fiancé!), Declan.

I'd also like to thank Declan's mum, Fay, who looked after our dogs so I could concentrate on writing the final chapters! Who would have thought those two little characters could be so distracting?

Thank you to everyone at the ANZIC-RC, who were the best colleagues anyone could ask for during a huge time of my life and were so excited for me throughout my writing journey.

I was fortunate enough to grow up in a beautiful small town where many people helped me become the writer I am today, including my parents, my sister Becky and my brother Josh. I would also like to say a special thankyou to my teachers, who supported me greatly in developing my writing skills and were always happy to help me learn more.

Who would have thought that shortly after all the ups and downs of writing a book, I'd be receiving a marriage proposal? Dec – you've been my biggest supporter and the greatest help throughout this journey. Thank you so much for reading rough drafts, for boosting my spirits and for encouraging me to stay on track (I know I didn't always seem grateful at the time for that!). Thank you for taking the photographs for the covers of *The Mindful Kind*. Thank you for understanding why I was in my pyjamas on the couch with my laptop for days at a time. I promise to start wearing real clothes again now!

To Simone, Terence, Emily, Claudia and Christina – sharing your experiences of mindfulness has been such a privilege and I can't thank you enough for being so thoughtful and open.

I will always be grateful to all my podcast listeners, who tune in each week, leave lovely reviews and share *The Mindful Kind* podcast with their friends and family. When I first launched *The Mindful Kind* back in 2015, I had no idea what I was doing or where podcasting could take me. Nearly three million downloads later, I've had the incredible opportunity to write this book and I can't ever tell you how much I appreciate every single one of you. Thank you.

Breathing techniques and meditations

Breathing techniques

Mindful breathing

Simply notice the journey of your breath as it moves in and out of your body. There's no need to change your breathing patterns or to deepen your breath, just notice it the way it is. You may also like to move your attention to one area of your body where you can particularly feel your breath, such as your nostrils or chest. Rest your attention on the area, noticing the subtle movements created by each breath. Whenever your mind wanders, bring your attention back to your breath.

The point of stillness

Take a few moments to bring your attention into the now, perhaps checking in with your own thoughts and feelings and the world around you. You might notice sounds, sights, what you can taste or smell and any sensations (such as the texture of materials against your skin). When it feels right for you, move your focus to your breath, just noticing as it flows in and out of your body.

Begin paying attention to the natural pause at the end of each exhale; the point of stillness. You don't need to elongate this pause or change it in any way, just notice its presence.

Continue with this practice as long as you like, perhaps a few minutes or a little longer. Your mind will likely wander (and that's perfectly okay!), so gently refocus on the practice whenever you can.

Three-part breathing

Take a deep breath in and hold it for a brief moment, then allow approximately 30 per cent of your breath to be exhaled from your stomach area. Hold the breath for another brief moment, then exhale another 30 per cent of the breath from your rib area. Hold the remainder of the breath once more and then exhale completely.

Breathing stairs

Imagine your breath is climbing a set of stairs. As you inhale, visualise your breath travelling up the vertical part of the stair, and as you exhale, visualise your breath travelling along the horizontal part of the stair. You can also explore what it feels like to imagine your breath is going down a set of stairs, instead of up!

You might like to experiment with the idea of climbing towards something, such as calm, relaxation, or peaceful sleep. This can be particularly useful if you're not quite feeling ready for sleep, or if you're in a state that isn't particularly conducive for good sleep (such as if you're stressed or feeling overwhelmed).

Breathing into the body

To begin, bring your attention to your feet. Inhale. As you exhale, imagine all the tension releasing from your feet, allowing them to sink into a state of relaxation.

Complete this same process throughout your whole body, moving from your feet, to your lower legs, upper legs, pelvic region and buttocks, stomach, lower back, chest, upper back, shoulders, upper arms, lower arms and wrists, hands, neck, head and face. You can move through the body quite quickly and make your way back down again, or take more time to explore each area of the body. For example, rather than sending your breath into your feet, you could begin with the toes of one foot, then the top of the foot, arch, heel and ankle.

Circular breathing

Imagine your breath is travelling around a circular shape, perhaps moving down one side of the shape as you exhale and moving up the other side of the shape as you inhale. Focus on smoothing out your breathing and reducing the pauses in between the inhalations and exhalations.

Meditations

Body scan

A body scan involves finding a comfortable, safe space where you can sit or lie down quietly. The aim of this practice is to simply notice each part of your body, without changing anything or being judgemental.

You can begin by taking your awareness to your toes or the top of your head. For example, you may notice your toes, then the balls of your feet, the arches of your feet, your heels, the tops of your feet, your lower legs, knees, and so on. Continue to move your awareness through your body, all the way up to the top of your head. You can do this practice quickly (if you only have a short amount of time) or you can slow it down and focus on each body part in depth. For example, you could focus on your hand as a whole, or explore your right wrist, the palm of your right hand, the back of your right hand, your right knuckles, each finger (one at a time) and each fingernail.

Once you've scanned your awareness through your body, you can spend some time focusing on your body as a whole, and then end the meditation when you feel ready.

Take a moment to lie down or sit comfortably with your spine fairly straight, and close your eyes. You may like to spend some time bringing yourself into the present moment by tuning in to your senses, noticing your breath and settling yourself into the environment around you.

When you're ready, take your attention down to the tips of your toes. Allow your attention to rest there for a moment.

Move your focus to the rest of your toes, then the arches of your feet, your heels and the tops of your feet.

Notice your ankles and lower legs. See if you can feel their weight, sinking into the furniture or floor.

Bring your attention to your knees and the backs of your knees, exploring any sensations there.

Feel the strong muscles in the top parts of your leg, including your hamstrings, quadriceps and inner thighs.

Move your focus to your groin, pelvis, hips and glutes.

Continue moving your attention further up your lower stomach, noticing your bellybutton. Observe any sensations there.

Rest your focus for a moment on your ribs and chest. You might like to explore the soft movements of these areas as they rise and fall with each breath.

Bring your attention to your right shoulder. Allow your attention to trickle down your right arm, noticing your upper arm, then your elbow, your lower arm and wrist. Explore the palm of your right hand and the back of your hand, then try to notice each finger, one by one. Your little finger, ring finger, middle finger, index finger and your thumb. You may even notice your fingernails.

Slowly, allow your attention to flow back up your right arm to your shoulder, across your chest and over to the left shoulder.

Begin to move your focus down your left arm, starting with your upper arm, then your elbow, your lower arm and wrist.

Notice the palm of your left hand and the back of your hand. Bring your attention to your left little finger, ring finger, middle finger, index finger and thumb. Try to notice each of your fingernails.

Gently allow your attention to move back up your arm and when it reaches your shoulder, feel that attention flowing over your upper back and lower back, like a wave washing over the sand.

Imagine your spine like a string of pearls and bring your attention to the bottom of the string of pearls, just at your tailbone. With each breath, move your focus slowly up your spine, taking all the time you need. When you reach the top, take a few easy, soft breaths, feeling the entirety of your back.

Invite your attention to continue moving up your neck, to the back of your head. See if you can notice the sides of your head and the top of your head. If you are lying down, you may notice the contact of your head with the floor or furniture, or maybe you can simply feel the support of your neck, holding your head up.

Move your attention to your forehead, eyebrows and temples. Notice your eyes and eyelids and explore the sensations of all the little muscles here. Feel your cheeks and nose, your upper lip, lower lip and your tongue, resting heavily in your mouth.

Notice the lower part of your jaw, the upper part of your jaw and your ears.

Take a few more easy breaths and begin to sense your body as a whole. Your entire body resting heavily, perhaps feeling a sensation of relaxation and support.

You may like to spend a few moments observing these sensations.

When you're ready, bring your attention back to the room by noticing what you can hear, taste, smell or feel. You may notice your breath by following the journey of each inhale and exhale. Take as much time as you like to slowly open your eyes and notice everything around you.

Meditation for self-love

Find somewhere quiet to sit and spend a little bit of time getting comfortable. When you feel ready, close your eyes.

Begin to bring your attention into the present moment by noticing:

- the connection between your body and the floor
- the sounds in the room around you and further away
- any tastes or aromas
- areas of tension and relaxation in your body, plus areas of warmth and coolness
- how you're feeling emotionally.

Once you feel more grounded and connected with the present moment, do a gentle scan through your body, noticing each body part from the top of your head all the way down to the tips of your toes.

Now allow a kind and positive thought about yourself to float into your awareness. It may take a little bit of time and you may notice a variety of different thoughts before you settle on one that resonates.

A few examples might be:

- I appreciate my individuality.
- I love the person I am.
- I embrace myself and everything that makes me who I am.
- I admire both my strengths and my weaknesses.
- I am proud of myself.

Once you have a kind and positive thought in your mind, try to immerse yourself in the meaning of it. For example, explore what it feels like to be proud of yourself. Notice where you can feel that emotion in your body. It might help to bring to mind someone else you're proud of and transfer your affection for them towards yourself.

You may feel challenged during this meditation, and that's perfectly okay! Let go of any unnecessary thoughts and refocus on either your positive thoughts, or take a break by noticing your breath.

When you feel ready, you can bring your attention back to the room, noticing all your senses and how you feel.

Soothing touch

Place one hand over the part of your body where you feel the most stress. For me, this tends to be my chest or stomach. Notice the warmth of your hand and the gentle pressure of it against your body. If it feels soothing to you, feel free to gently rub the area in small circles, or imagine a warm light emanating from your hand into that stressed area of your body. If you choose to picture the warm light, you can also experiment with visualising the stress melting away from the area; you might picture it as a dark sticky substance like tar that will melt and dissolve, or a hot red liquid that evaporates and disappears).

Progressive muscle relaxation

The aim of this strategy is to systematically isolate and tense your muscles and then release the tension while paying close attention to the sensation of relaxation.

For example, you might start with your feet by squeezing all the muscles in that area and then releasing them. You can continue up your entire body – your lower legs, upper legs, groin and buttocks, stomach, chest, upper back, upper arms, lower arms and hands. You can then do one final squeeze using your entire body and allow yourself to sink into the floor or seat, becoming heavy and relaxed.

Alternatively, you can choose particular muscles that you know often tense up when you're stressed, and focus on deliberately tensing and relaxing them.

Be careful not to tense your muscles so much that you feel pain or discomfort – the aim is simply to experience a sense of relaxation.

Meditation for self-compassion

Find a comfortable space to sit quietly. Start becoming grounded in the present moment by doing some mindful breathing or a short body scan, or tune in to each of your senses. You may also like to close your eyes.

When you feel ready, start to observe your emotions – without judgement. Simply notice how you're feeling. For example, you might notice that you're feeling hurt, sad, guilty, stressed or angry. There may be a whole constellation of emotions.

Begin to imagine some kind words you would say to a friend if they were experiencing all your present emotions. How would you comfort them? What would you say to ensure they felt loved and supported?

Now begin to direct those kind words to yourself and your emotions.

Practise speaking to yourself in a compassionate way and acknowledge all your emotions with kindness and open-mindedness.

It can also help to imagine yourself holding each of your emotions in your hands and gently exploring each one – what they look like and feel like.

Once you've finished compassionately exploring your emotions, bring your attention back to the room and open your eyes.